Taxcafe.co.uk Tax Guides

Coronavirus Tax Planning

By Carl Bayley BSc FCA
and
Nick Braun PhD

Important Legal Notices:

Taxcafe®
Tax Guide - "Coronavirus Tax Planning"

Published by:
Taxcafe UK Limited
67 Milton Road
Kirkcaldy KY1 1TL
Tel: (0044) 01592 560081
Email: team@taxcafe.co.uk

1st edition, March 2020

ISBN 978-1-911020-54-7

Disclaimer
Before reading or relying on the content of this tax guide please read the disclaimer carefully.

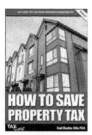

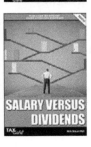

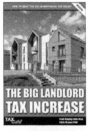

Disclaimer

1. This guide is intended as **general guidance** only and does NOT constitute accountancy, tax, investment or other professional advice.

2. The authors and Taxcafe UK Limited make no representations or warranties with respect to the accuracy or completeness of this publication and cannot accept any responsibility or liability for any loss or risk, personal or otherwise, which may arise, directly or indirectly, from reliance on information contained in this publication.

3. Please note that tax legislation, the law and practices of Government and regulatory authorities (e.g. HM Revenue & Customs) are constantly changing. We therefore recommend that for accountancy, tax, investment or other professional advice, you consult a suitably qualified accountant, tax advisor, financial adviser, or other professional adviser.

4. Please also note that your personal circumstances may vary from the general examples provided in this guide and your professional adviser will be able to provide specific advice based on your personal circumstances.

5. This guide covers UK taxation only and any references to 'tax' or 'taxation', unless the contrary is expressly stated, refer to UK taxation only. Please note that references to the 'UK' do not include the Channel Islands or the Isle of Man. Foreign tax implications are beyond the scope of this guide.

6. All persons described in the examples in this guide are entirely fictional. Any similarities to actual persons, living or dead, or to fictional characters created by any other author, are entirely coincidental.

7. The views expressed in this publication are the authors' own personal views and do not necessarily reflect the views of any organisation which they may represent.

About the Authors & Taxcafe

Carl Bayley is the author of a series of Taxcafe guides designed specifically for the layman. Carl's particular speciality is his ability to take the weird, complex and inexplicable world of taxation and set it out in the kind of clear, straightforward language taxpayers themselves can understand. As he often says himself, "my job is to translate 'tax' into English".

In addition to being a recognised author, Carl has often spoken about taxation on radio and television, including the BBC's *It's Your Money* programme and the Jeremy Vine Show on Radio 2.

A chartered accountant by training, Carl was Chairman of the Tax Faculty of the Institute of Chartered Accountants in England and Wales from 2015 to 2018 and has been a member of the Institute's governing Council since 2007.

Nick Braun founded Taxcafe.co.uk in 1999, along with his partner, Aileen Smith. As the driving force behind the company, their aim is to provide affordable plain-English tax information to private individuals, investors, business owners and professional advisors.

Since then Taxcafe has become one of the best-known tax publishers in the UK and has won several business awards.

Nick has been involved in the tax publishing world since 1989 as a writer, editor and publisher. He holds a doctorate in economics from the University of Glasgow, where he was awarded the prestigious William Glen Scholarship and later became a Research Fellow. Prior to that, he graduated with distinction from the University of South Africa, the country's oldest university, earning the highest results in economics in the university's history.

Contents

Introduction

At this difficult time the authors and Taxcafe would like to offer our very best wishes to all of our customers and their families and friends.

We are going through unprecedented times and all of us are struggling to find new ways to deal with the world we now find ourselves in. Even tax is affected by the Coronavirus. That is why we have launched this special guide to help you understand the impact the current crisis will have on your tax obligations; how normal, sensible, tax planning measures may be affected; and what you can do to protect yourself, your business, and your family financially.

We have included a broad range of measures and advice for all types of business including: sole traders; partnerships; landlords; and companies and their owners; as well as individuals reviewing their pensions and other tax-efficient investments; and families wishing to help each other with cash gifts or property transfers. We even have some advice for bored employees stuck at home who manage to turn a hobby into a business.

We start by summarising the emergency measures and extra help available to business owners during the crisis. While this is most welcome (and essential), we know there will be a price to pay later, so we have taken a look at some of the future tax increases we may potentially see in the future.

Following that, we turn our attention to company directors and look at what planning measures you can implement to help both you and your company survive the storm. Issues such as how much cash to take out of the business, whether to pay it back in, and what form it should take, are examined, as well as crucial non-cash transactions that need to be formalised now to help you save tax in the long run.

Then we move to some general issues relevant to every type of business: how to save tax by employing your children (perhaps a good way to keep them occupied while schools, colleges and universities are closed); what happens if you defer capital expenditure, will you still get as much tax relief; and what can you claim if you are forced to work from home more than usual, or even for the first time.

We look at pensions and other tax-efficient investments and consider how the changed circumstances we are experiencing affect key decisions. Should pension contributions be postponed to save cash, will you get more tax relief if you make contributions in a future tax year instead, what happens if you withdraw money from your pension now?

Then we move on to unincorporated businesses: sole traders, partnerships (including LLPs), and landlords operating as individuals: what we might broadly call the 'self-employed'. The tax system for the self-employed is undoubtedly complex and we explore how it works, how accounting periods relate to tax years and, more importantly, to tax payments. Cashflow is critical at the moment and we never forget that when we look at the impact of tax planning measures in this guide.

Among other crucial points, we will see how 31st January 2021 is likely to be a very bad day for many taxpayers, with huge tax bills arising in many cases: and we will, of course, see what can be done to reduce or postpone those bills.

We will explore the potential benefits of changing your accounting date. Under the right conditions, this can enable a sole trader or business partner to reduce current tax bills **and** stack up extra tax relief for the future; it can effectively enable you to get tax relief on trading losses twice; or it can provide early relief for tax saving benefits you've stacked up in the past: and now could be the best time to do it!

We then move onto the key topic of 'marginal rate planning': how moving taxable income from one tax year to another can save significant amounts of tax. Several chapters are devoted to this important subject, which is relevant to all types of self-employed business owners (and to company directors, but we covered them earlier). We will examine the action you can take both before and after your accounting date and we will look at both the cashflow savings and the ultimate, overall, savings you can generate.

Sometimes just deferring tax can be beneficial, especially when cash is tight, so we will also look at how to use the same techniques to simply defer taxable profits. This applies equally to companies, even though their tax rate is not set to change in the foreseeable future. For the self-employed, there are significant potential cashflow savings to be made, although the payment on account system can also lead to some surprising consequences.

In some cases, absolute, long-term savings can be achieved by accelerating taxable income into an earlier year. This creates a trade off between a short-term cashflow disadvantage and a long-term saving, but we explain how, if you can afford it, this can be a pretty good investment.

Cashflow and tax planning are often in conflict and many business owners may be concerned that putting off some of their expenditure will lead to higher tax bills. We look at what spending can safely be deferred without the risk of giving yourself a bigger tax bill.

Some people suffering sharp falls in sales might wonder if it would be a good idea to deregister for VAT. We look at the technicalities involved and the pros and cons. We also look at VAT relief for bad debts.

Next, we look at the cash basis available to landlords and small trading businesses. We compare and contrast these with traditional accounting and look at the pros and cons. For landlords, we see how the cash basis may be incredibly helpful in dealing with voids or rent arrears; for all types of self-employed taxpayers we look at the savings that can be generated by joining or leaving the cash basis at the right time.

Incorporation (transferring your business into a company) is often a good long-term tax planning strategy but can come at an 'upfront cost'. In a special chapter devoted to the subject, we explain why this may be the best time to go ahead and do it.

Company accounting dates work differently to self-employed taxpayers in the self-assessment system but nonetheless there can still be advantages to changing your accounting date when company profits have suffered a severe reduction. We explain how.

Many businesses will sadly be making losses at present. The rules on loss relief vary tremendously, depending on the type of business and the legal structure it is held in. We examine the rules for companies, unincorporated trading businesses (sole traders, partnerships and LLPs), and landlords, including the badly-stricken furnished holiday letting sector. We explain the reliefs available and how to make the most of them. The chapter on furnished holiday lets also contains advice on how to maintain the special tax status that these businesses enjoy during the current crisis.

Moving into more personal and family tax-planning areas, we look at why this could be a good time to make property transfers to children, other family members, or heirs. We also look at whether it makes sense to crystallise capital losses and how to make the most of them if you do.

With many people helping out their family through cash gifts, we look at how to make sure these are done tax-efficiently.

On the way, we pick up a few other issues like the different tax rates for Scottish taxpayers and the child benefit charge, including a reminder that those who may able to claim child benefit again this year without losing it through the tax system should remember to do so.

Lastly, we finish with a look at how to turn a hobby into extra tax-free income while you're in lockdown. Maybe it could be the start of something big?

We've done our best to pack this guide with useful advice for all types of businesses and individual taxpayers and help everyone get through this crisis.

When it comes to tax, we believe you should never pay more than your fair share, and you have every right to undertake sensible planning measures to legitimately reduce, or delay, your tax bills; especially to protect your business, your family, or both.

However, when all is said and done, the reason we pay tax is to fund vital public services, something that is now more important than ever. Tax is the hallmark of civilisation and while we will help you to pay no more than your fair share, we still urge everyone, now, more than ever, to pay your tax!

Finally, we leave you with this thought:

> Stay safe,
> Keep well,
> Tell corona,
> 'Go to Hell'

Take care everyone and **_please_** remember to observe Government guidelines on social distancing, etc, for the safely of us all.

All the Best from Carl & Nick

Scope of this Guide & Words of Explanation

It is possible that further changes will be announced that affect some of the information contained in this guide.

Although the guide covers a fair amount of ground, it does not cover every possible scenario – that would be impossible without making it much longer and possibly much more difficult to digest.

There are also *non-tax* factors that have to be considered when taking action to reduce your tax bill. In some instances other considerations will outweigh any potential tax savings.

For all of these reasons it is vital that you obtain professional advice before taking any action based on information contained in this guide. The authors and Taxcafe UK Ltd cannot accept any responsibility for any loss which may arise as a consequence of any action taken, or any decision to refrain from taking action, as a result of reading this guide.

Throughout this guide, unless stated to the contrary, all examples, calculations, tables, etc, are based on the following assumptions:

i)   Individuals are UK resident and domiciled
ii)   Companies are UK resident
iii)   Individuals are not Scottish taxpayers
iv)   Individuals are not subject to the child benefit charge
v)   Individuals are not claiming the marriage allowance
vi)   Individuals are below state pension age

Furthermore, 'spouses' include civil partners but only include spouses who are legally married (or legally registered civil partners).

Scottish taxpayers pay Income Tax at different rates to the rest of the UK. These are covered in Chapter 27. The Welsh Assembly also has powers to vary Income Tax rates for Welsh taxpayers but has not yet done so.

To keep things simple, we will also largely ignore Student Loan Repayments (unless expressly stated to the contrary). These are generally collected through the tax system (either PAYE or self-assessment) but are not, strictly speaking, a tax.

Some Words of Explanation

In this guide, we are aiming to provide as much helpful advice to as many business owners and private individuals as possible. Accordingly, we are going to cover a wide range of topics and it is important for readers to understand some of the terminology we will use to distinguish which bits of advice apply in your own circumstances. Hence:

An '**unincorporated business**' means a sole trader, a partnership, or an individual landlord renting out property. It covers both trading businesses and property letting businesses.

A '**trading business**' does not include property letting businesses or other forms of what HMRC classes as 'investment businesses' (e.g. investing on the stock market). However, it does include professions (accountants, lawyers, doctors, dentists, surveyors, architects, vets, etc). There is seldom any difference in the tax treatment of a trade or a profession, except in the case of 'early years loss relief' for members of an LLP (see Chapter 36).

An '**LLP**' means a Limited Liability Partnership. These are generally treated the same as any other partnership for tax purposes, except where we have highlighted otherwise.

'**Earned income**' in tax terminology means employment income or self-employment or partnership trading income.

The '**tax year**' means the UK tax year, running from 6th April in one calendar year to 5th April in the next. For example, the year from 6th April 2020 to 5th April 2021 is the 2020/21 tax year.

Chapter 1

Government Support for Business

The Government has announced a huge package of support for businesses during the Coronavirus Crisis:

Job Retention Scheme

Under this scheme employers can claim a grant covering 80% of the salary of a "furloughed" employee, subject to a cap of £2,500 a month. Employers can top up salaries beyond this if they wish.

An online portal to make claims is expected to be available by the end of April 2020.

Claims must be for a minimum of three weeks and the scheme is expected to last for at least three months, backdated to 1 March 2020.

The Government will also cover the employer's national insurance and minimum auto-enrolment pension scheme contributions associated with these capped salaries. Fees, commissions and bonuses are not included.

The scheme covers the following individuals:

- Full-time employees, part-time employees, employees on agency contracts and employees on flexible or zero-hour contracts.

- Employees on your payroll on or before 28 February 2020

- Employees made redundant after 28 February 2020 but re-hired and placed on furlough

(The Government seems to have forgotten that this February was a leap year with 29 days!)

If an employee is still working but on reduced hours or for reduced pay, they are not eligible for the Job Retention Scheme.

Employees on sick leave or self-isolating should get statutory sick pay, but can be furloughed after this.

Employees who are shielding in line with public health guidance because they are in a high risk category can be placed on furlough.

A business does not have to place all of its employees on furlough.

What is a Furloughed Employee?

A furloughed employee is one who, instead of being made redundant, remains employed but is placed on a leave of absence because the employer can't operate, or there isn't enough work for the employee to do because of coronavirus.

An employee's consent may be necessary before changing their status to furloughed with reduced pay (although this consent will probably be forthcoming if the alternative is redundancy). An employee's status is subject to employment law and what is set out in their contract of employment.

Some employers have a contractual right to lay off workers without pay when there isn't any work for them to do. Most employees, however, have the right to be paid their full salaries if they are willing and able to work, even if their employer cannot provide them with any.

To be eligible for the Government subsidy the employer should write to the employee confirming that they have been furloughed and keep a record of this communication.

The key point is that the employee cannot do any work at all for the employer while furloughed, including answering emails.

No doubt when the dust settles from coronavirus, HMRC will spend many years clawing back erroneous and fraudulent payments under the Job Retention Scheme.

According to the Treasury, those who pay themselves a salary and dividends through their own company will be covered for their *salary* by the scheme.

However, we think the Treasury is simply paying lip service to company owners here, especially owners of one-man band companies. The vast majority will not qualify for the scheme because they will find it impossible to furlough themselves and remain completely inactive. Most directors have to actively manage their businesses in some way on a daily basis, sometimes 7 days a week.

To qualify for the scheme they would have to ignore all calls and emails from customers and suppliers and would not be able to make any plans to prepare the business for the end of the coronavirus pandemic. What nonsense!

Employees can complete training courses while furloughed. In this case their pay must be at least the national minimum wage or living wage.

80% of What?

Salaries as of 28 February 2020 should be used to calculate the 80%.

For employees whose pay varies, the 80% is calculated using the *higher* of:

- The same month's earnings from the previous year, or
- Average monthly earnings from the 2019/20 tax year

If the employee has been employed for less than a year the claim can be based on an average of their monthly earnings since they started work.

Tax Treatment

Salaries of furloughed employees are subject to income tax and national insurance as usual and employees will also pay automatic enrolment contributions as usual.

Employers are liable to pay employer's national insurance and automatic enrolment contributions as usual.

The grant payments received by the business are included in its taxable profits and the business will be allowed a deduction for the payments to employees, as is normally the case with salaries.

Self-employment Income Support Scheme

This scheme is open to sole traders and business partners. Those who run their businesses through a limited company are not self employed and can not claim this grant.

It provides a taxable grant worth 80% of your trading profits up to a maximum of £2,500 per month for at least 3 months. The grant is taxable.

HMRC will contact you if you are eligible for the scheme and invite you to apply online.

To qualify you must:

- Have submitted your 2018/19 tax return (the one that was due by 31 January 2020). If you haven't completed it, you have until 23 April 2020.

- Have traded in the tax year 2019/20 (the one that ended on 5 April 2020)

- Be trading when you apply, or would be except for coronavirus

- Have lost trading profits due to coronavirus

Furthermore, only those with profits of less than £50,000 will qualify. Furthermore, more than half of your income must come from self employment. To meet these requirements one of the following conditions must hold true:

- 2018/19 trading profits less than £50,000, these profits are more than half your total taxable income

- 2016/17, 2017/18, 2018/19 average trading profits less than £50,000, these profits are more than half of your average taxable income

If you weren't trading for all three of those years, HMRC will only use those years for which you filed a tax return.

How Much Will I Get?

HMRC will add together the total trading profits for the following three tax years (where applicable)

- 2016/17
- 2017/18
- 2018/19

This will then be divided by three to calculate the average annual profit.

The average profit is then divided by 12 to get a monthly amount.

This will then be capped at £2,500 per month for 3 months.

The whole grant will be paid directly into your bank account in one instalment.

Income Tax Payments on Account

Payments on account due by 31 July 2020 can be deferred until 31 January 2021.

The deferment is optional. You can make the payments at any time before 31 January 2021.

This is an automatic offer and no application is required. No penalties or interest for late payment will be charged if you defer payment until January 2021.

VAT Deferral

The Government has announced a VAT payments deferral to help businesses experiencing cash-flow problems during the coronavirus pandemic.

All businesses can defer VAT payments that are due between 20 March 2020 and 30 June 2020.

You will then have until 31 March 2021 to pay any VAT deferred as a result of this announcement.

VAT returns do, however, still have to be submitted on time.

You do not need to inform HMRC if you wish to defer payment. You can simply not make VAT payments due in this period.

Those who pay by direct debit should cancel these with their bank. This can usually be done online but you must make sure you do this before HMRC attempts to automatically collect payment when it receives your VAT return.

Remember, you will have to reinstate your direct debit for payments that fall due after 30 June 2020.

You don't have to defer your VAT payments and can continue to make payments as normal. HMRC will also continue to pay repayment claims as normal.

Business Rates

The Government has announced a huge package to help with business rates:

- Businesses in the retail, hospitality and leisure sectors will enjoy a complete business rates holiday for 2020/21. This will cover shops, restaurants, pubs, clubs, and cinemas. No action is required to claim relief.

- Retail, hospitality and leisure businesses that occupy a property with a rateable value of between £15,000 and less than £51,000 are eligible for a £25,000 grant. Properties with a rateable value of up to £15,000 will be eligible for a £10,000 grant. Your local authority is supposed to write to you if you are eligible but you can go onto their websites now for details of how to apply, where applicable.

- Certain nursery businesses will enjoy a complete business rates holiday for 2020/21.

- Business that already pay little or no business rates because of small business rates relief or rural rate relief are entitled to a £10,000 grant. Your local authority is supposed to write to you if you are eligible but you can go onto their websites now for details of how to apply, where applicable.

Because some elements of business support are devolved, the measures you can access may differ if your business is in Scotland, Wales or Northern Ireland.

Statutory Sick Pay

The Government is introducing legislation to allow small and medium-sized businesses (fewer than 250 employees) to reclaim Statutory Sick Pay (SSP) paid for sickness absence due to coronavirus.

The refund will cover SSP for up to two weeks.

Employers should maintain records of staff absences and payments of SSP, but employees will not need a note from a GP.

The Government is currently working on setting up the repayment mechanism.

Business Interruption Loan Scheme

This scheme provides small and medium-sized businesses access to loans, overdrafts, invoice finance and asset finance of up to £5 million for up to six years.

The Government will also make a Business Interruption Payment to cover the first 12 months of interest payments and any bank fees, so smaller businesses will benefit from no upfront costs and lower initial repayments.

The Government is also providing banks with a guarantee of 80% on each loan to give them confidence to led to smaller businesses.

There are 40 accredited lenders able to offer the scheme, including all the major banks.

Time to Pay

All businesses and self-employed people in financial distress, and with outstanding tax liabilities, may be eligible to receive support with their tax affairs through HMRC's Time to Pay service.

These arrangements are agreed on a case-by-case basis.

If you've missed a tax payment or you fear you might miss your next payment due to coronavirus there is a dedicated helpline: 0800 0159 559.

Commercial Tenants – Protection from Eviction

Commercial tenants who cannot pay their rent because of coronavirus are being protected from eviction.

This measure means no business will automatically forfeit its lease and be evicted if it misses a payment up until 30 June.

The Government can extend this period if needed.

This is not a rental holiday. All commercial tenants remain liable for their rent.

Chapter 2

Future Tax Increases

The Government has thrown huge resources at supporting individuals and businesses during the Coronavirus outbreak. We at Taxcafe fully endorse these measures because they aim to reduce financial hardship and protect the economy from the long-term damage that would be caused by mass unemployment and good businesses having to shut their doors permanently.

Not all of the Government support is direct spending. For example, the £330 billion of business loan guarantees will only result in increased Government spending to the extent that the loans are not repaid.

And allowing businesses to postpone paying VAT and individuals to postpone their July 2020 payments on account does not amount to a tax cut but a tax deferral.

However, there have been some huge handouts announced including the Coronavirus Job Retention Scheme, the Coronavirus Self-employment Income Support Scheme, and a huge package to help with business rates, including cash grants of up to £25,000.

We can probably expect more handouts to be announced in the weeks and months ahead.

This huge surge in spending will be financed through increased borrowing but as pointed out by Robert Chote, head of the Office for Budget Responsibility, now is not the time to be squeamish about adding to the public debt, as was the case during the Second World War.

The Government may be able to get away with borrowing huge sums of money because interest rates are so low at present. It can currently borrow money for 10 years and pay less than 0.5% interest per year.

As long as the Government can continue to pay the interest on its debt there will not be an immediate crisis but eventually there will have to be a reckoning and this will probably mean higher taxes.

In their 2019 election manifesto the Conservative Party promised not to raise the rates of income tax, national insurance or VAT. This promise will probably have to be broken, given the extraordinary times we find ourselves in. In any case, there are lots of other ways the Government can raise tax.

It's likely that any such taxes will target higher income earners and those with assets. We can expect politicians to start using that phrase "it's only fair that those with the broadest shoulders pay a little more," as they did during the 2008 financial crisis.

Broader tax increases should also be expected. Chancellor Rishi Sunak has already stated everyone will have to "chip in" to right the ship.

We have no idea what shape any such tax increases would take or when they would be introduced. But it's important, when planning your tax affairs to keep one eye on the future as well.

Future tax increases could include:

Freezing the Higher-rate Threshold
The higher-rate threshold was £45,000 back in 2017/18 and has increased by more than the rate of inflation to £50,000 today. The Government could therefore argue that freezing the threshold for several years is justifiable.

Freezing tax thresholds is the easiest way for governments to increase taxes without telling anyone.

Increasing Dividend Tax Rates
Dividend tax rates were increased by 7.5% in 2016 to clamp down on company owners who take most of their income as dividends and pay little or no national insurance.

There would be little sympathy from the wider public if shareholders were once again forced to pay more tax. We wouldn't be surprised to see tax rates increase by 2.5 percentage points at some point.

Scrapping the Dividend Allowance
The dividend allowance was reduced from £5,000 to £2,000 in 2018. It could be reduced to, say, £1,000 or scrapped altogether, although we don't think this is likely because of the increased admin burden it would place on HMRC.

Increasing the Additional Rate
The additional rate was reduced from 50% to 45% in 2013. Increasing the rate back to 50% would be much easier than raising the 20% basic rate or 40% higher rate. The additional rate for dividend income is currently 38.1% and that could be raised too.

A Penny (or Two) on Income Tax
During the 2019 general election the Liberal Democrats pledged to increase all income tax rates by 1% to raise money for the NHS. They said this would raise £7 billion a year. Such a tax increase would be more politically palatable for a Conservative Government following the coronavirus outbreak.

Increasing National Insurance Rates
At present salary earners, sole traders and business partners pay 2% national insurance on income over £50,000. This rate could be increased to help fund the NHS and to help fund other state benefits if the public finances come under pressure.

On income below £50,000 self-employed people currently pay 9% national insurance compared with the 12% paid by salary earners. We can expect the rates for self-employed business owners to be brought in line with those of salary earners. Chancellor Rishi Sunak has already hinted that this will happen.

Reducing Pension Tax Relief
Higher-rate tax relief on pension contributions is estimated to cost the Government roughly £10 billion per year. For many years now commentators in the pensions industry have feared that it will be taken away and replaced with basic-rate tax relief on all pension contributions.

There were rumours circulating that an announcement would be made in the March 2020 Budget by Sajid Javid, before he resigned as Chancellor of the Exchequer. No changes were announced by the current Chancellor Rishi Sunak.

Scrapping higher-rate tax relief altogether would take away much of the incentive to save into a pension (unless you also enjoy a generous contribution from your employer).

A far easier short-term change would be to reduce the annual allowance (the amount you can contribute each year) from £40,000 to perhaps £30,000 or £20,000.

Scrapping Entrepreneurs Relief
Entrepreneurs Relief allows you to pay just 10% capital gains tax when you sell your business or wind it up. In the March 2020 Budget the lifetime limit was reduced from £10 million of capital gains to just £1 million. We wouldn't rule out a further reduction or even a complete scrapping of this tax relief.

Increasing Capital Gains Tax
We also wouldn't rule out increases in capital gains tax generally because people with assets are likely to be an easy political target. At present higher-rate taxpayers pay 28% capital gains tax when they sell residential property and 20% when they sell other assets. These rates could be increased fairly significantly at the stroke of a pen.

Inheritance Tax
Changes to inheritance tax have been widely mooted following a report by the Office of Tax Simplification. However, there was no mention of any changes in the March 2020 Budget.

The inheritance tax nil rate band has been frozen at its current level of £325,000 since 6 April 2009. In the absence of a major overhaul of the grave robbers tax the £325,000 exemption could be frozen for much longer.

And because people with significant assets are an easy political target, it would be fairly easy to introduce a tax rate higher than the current 40% for larger estates.

Stamp Duty Land Tax
Because people who buy expensive assets are another easy political target we wouldn't rule out increases in the stamp duty land tax paid on expensive properties.

VAT

The Government has frozen the VAT registration threshold at £85,000 until 31st March 2022.

The Office of Tax Simplification has also called for an overhaul of the threshold and we suspect they would like to see a drastic reduction in the threshold on the grounds that a high threshold limits the amount of work small businesses take on.

In the absence of any big changes it would be fairly easy to keep the threshold at £85,000 to gradually drag more businesses into the tax net.

A Final Word on Potential Tax Increases

It's important to stress that all of the above is highly speculative. We do not know what tax policymakers have up their sleeves but we wouldn't be at all surprised if at least some of these measures are introduced in the years ahead.

We're also not making any moral judgements about whether any such tax increases would be right or wrong. The country's finances will be in a terrible state when we get through the coronavirus pandemic, as will the finances of many taxpayers who may wish to do what they can to protect their families.

Chapter 3

Company Directors: Salaries and Dividends

The coronavirus outbreak is an enormous economic shock which has resulted in an unprecedented shutdown of large parts of the economy.

As a result, many readers will expect their companies' profits to fall significantly. In many cases once profitable companies will become loss making.

In this chapter we hope to provide some ideas to help company owners protect their own cash and their companies' cash in the months ahead in order to safeguard their businesses and employees.

Tax-free Salaries

There are three relevant thresholds for the 2020/21 tax year:

- Employer's national insurance   £8,788
- Employee's national insurance   £9,500
- Income tax   £12,500

Where the company does not have any spare national insurance employment allowance, a salary of £9,500 is generally optimal where the director does not have income from other sources.

A small amount of employer's national insurance will be payable, compared with a completely tax-free salary of £8,788, but the extra corporation tax relief outweighs the national insurance cost.

If the company has spare employment allowance, a salary of £12,500 is generally more tax efficient. In some cases, however (when the company owner has significant income from other sources), sticking with a salary of £9,500 may be better from a tax saving standpoint.

Some older couples who are over state pension age and have no other employees may be able to receive a salary of up to £23,280 each with no national insurance liability at all.

In most cases company directors should continue to pay themselves these optimal salaries, wherever possible, because they provide corporation tax relief and are tax efficient for the directors too. It's a case of use them or lose them.

Furthermore, a salary of at least £6,240 is necessary to protect your state pension entitlement this year.

Most company owners will require these relatively small salaries to cover their living costs. But what if you want to keep the money in your company, for example to pay staff salaries?

There's nothing to stop you paying yourself a salary and lending the money back to the company later on. Alternatively you may decide to not withdraw the cash at all for now.

The general rule is that remuneration can only be deducted from the company's current taxable profits if it is 'paid' within nine months of the company's year end.

However, HMRC will accept that remuneration is paid when it is credited to the director's loan account.

So if you don't need the cash, there's nothing to stop you running your salary through the monthly payroll as normal and crediting the amounts to your director's loan account.

(Please note this is just a brief overview of company owner salaries. For a more detailed discussion see the Taxcafe guide *Salary versus Dividends*.)

Dividends

The first port of call is to take as much tax-free dividend income as you can. Every company owner can take a tax-free dividend of £2,000 per year thanks to the annual dividend allowance. Again, it's a case of use it or lose it.

Some company owners can pay themselves more tax-free dividend income if their salary does not use up all of their income tax personal allowance and they do not have any income from other sources.

Beyond that, choosing the right amount of dividend income to take this year may be a lot more complex.

Lending the Money Back to Your Company

It's important to stress that any dividend you pay yourself can be lent back to your company if the company's cash position deteriorates unexpectedly after the dividend has been paid.

In many cases dividends are declared but not paid out immediately. Instead they are credited to the director's loan account and withdrawn gradually during the year.

If you don't have other financial resources it will still be necessary to receive enough cash to settle your own income tax bill.

This will be a more significant issue for higher-rate taxpayers than basic-rate taxpayers. For example, a basic-rate taxpayer who takes a dividend of £30,000 over and above what is covered by their remaining personal allowance and dividend allowance will have an income tax bill of £2,250 (at 7.5%). This means £27,750 can be lent back to the company.

A higher-rate taxpayer who takes an additional dividend of £30,000 will have an income tax bill of £9,750 (at 32.5%) which means only £20,250 can be safely lent back to the company.

Distributable Profits

With many companies expecting to make smaller profits in the near term, it's important to remember that, under the Companies Act, a company cannot legally pay a dividend unless it has sufficient distributable profits to cover it.

If a dividend exceeds the company's distributable profits it will be unlawful and the company may be able to recover the amount from the director.

A company's distributable profits are its accumulated realised profits, less accumulated realised losses. This information can generally be found in the company's most recent annual accounts.

This means that it is not necessary for the company to actually make a profit in the year the dividend is paid, as long as there are sufficient accumulated profits (after tax) from previous years.

So all is not necessarily lost if you fear your company may move into loss in the months ahead. As long as there are sufficient distributable profits from previous years, it may be possible to continue paying dividends.

Where the most recent set of annual accounts do not show sufficient profits, interim accounts or management accounts can be prepared with more up to date information. This may be useful if business conditions have improved after the last set of accounts were prepared.

It's also important to remember that directors have a duty to promote the company's success, protect its assets and take reasonable action to ensure that the company can pay its debts. If future trading losses are expected, this is a factor that should be taken into account when considering the cash flow implications of any proposed dividend.

Thus, even if the most recent set of accounts show that there are sufficient distributable profits, the directors must take account of any change in the company's financial position since the accounts date and consider whether the company will remain solvent after any proposed dividend is paid. The key point is that directors must act honestly and reasonably at all times.

Dividends Taxed at 7.5%

This year a company owner who takes a salary of, say, £9,500 and does not have any income from other sources can take a tax-free dividend of £5,000 and additional dividend income of up to £35,500 taxed at 7.5%. The income tax payable on this additional dividend income will be £2,663.

The company owner will then have total taxable income of £50,000. Any more dividend income will be taxed at 32.5%.

If the company owner does have income from other sources, this will have to be factored into the equation. For example, a company owner who has salary and rental income of, say, £30,000 can take a tax-free dividend of £2,000 and additional dividend income of £18,000 taxed at 7.5%.

Subject to the caveats listed above, most company owners should probably continue paying themselves as much dividend income as they can taxed at just 7.5%.

This will help protect against:

- Future dividend tax increases
- Business risk
- Becoming a higher-rate taxpayer

It is possible (but not certain) that dividend tax rates will be increased again at some point in the future. Thus it may be better to withdraw as much income as you can now taxed at 7.5% in case the rate is increased to, say, 10%.

Some company owners may also wish to remove surplus cash from their companies to protect against business risk (arguably your money is at greater risk in the company's bank account than your own).

It may also be worth paying yourself the maximum dividend taxed at 7.5% if you think you may become a higher-rate taxpayer in the future.

In other words, it may be better to *definitely* pay 7.5% tax this year rather than *possibly* 32.5% or more in a future tax year.

Why would you expect to become a higher-rate taxpayer in the future? Perhaps you expect the profits of your business to grow or you expect to receive more income from other sources, e.g. an inheritance.

Although you may never become a higher-rate taxpayer, you arguably have very little to lose by paying yourself the maximum dividend taxed at 7.5%.

If you do become a higher-rate taxpayer you will save 25% (by paying 7.5% tax this year rather than 32.5% on the same money in a future tax year).

If you never become a higher-rate taxpayer you will probably lose nothing because you will pay 7.5% tax this year rather than 7.5% when you extract the same profits in a future tax year.

Dividends Taxed at 32.5%

Once you have £50,000 of taxable income (from your company and other sources) you will pay 32.5% income tax on any additional dividend income you receive.

Coupled with corporation tax, the total effective tax rate is 45%.

Company owners who normally receive dividends taxed at 32.5%, but are cautious about the current economic outlook, could consider reducing or halting altogether dividend income taxed at 32.5% this year.

Example

During the current 2020/21 tax year Lorna pays herself a salary of £9,500 and a dividend of £65,500 for a total taxable income of £75,000. She does not have any income from other sources.

The final £25,000 of her dividend income is taxed at 32.5%, producing an income tax bill of £8,125.

Next year (2021/22) Lorna finds that she can only pay herself a salary and dividend totalling £30,000. Assuming for simplicity that the higher-rate threshold is also £50,000 next year, this means that Lorna will effectively be wasting £20,000 of her basic-rate band next year.

But if she had been more cautious and taken £20,000 less dividend income this year (taxed at 32.5%) and then paid herself an additional £20,000 next year (taxed at just 7.5%), she could have saved herself £5,000 in tax.

Company owners can also consider simply postponing dividends taxed at 32.5% until much later in the tax year, when a clearer picture of business conditions may have emerged.

Dividends for the current 2020/21 tax year can be declared right up until 5 April 2021.

Bigger catch-up dividends can also be declared in a future tax year with no adverse tax penalty, as long as these do not take your taxable income over £100,000. Once your income exceeds £100,000, your personal allowance is gradually withdrawn. As explained in Chapter 13, the effective tax rate on dividend income in the £100,000-£125,000 tax bracket varies according to your circumstances but will often work out at 53.5%.

Example

Daniel is a company owner who normally pays himself a small salary and dividend totalling £100,000 each year. This year he decides to reduce his dividend income by £25,000 because of the uncertain economic outlook.

Next year he's more confident about the business outlook and pays himself his usual £100,000, plus an additional £25,000 to make up for his drop in income this year. This means his total taxable income will be £125,000 and his personal allowance will be completely withdrawn. Daniel will pay tax at an effective rate of 53.5% instead of the usual 32.5% on the additional catch-up dividend of £25,000.

The end result is Daniel will pay an additional £5,250 in income tax for acting prudently this year. For this reason he may wish to treat the current tax year as a year of austerity and not pay the catch-up dividend.

Avoiding the Child Benefit Charge

Once your income goes over £50,000, you start paying the child benefit charge if you are the highest earner in the household. Once your income reaches £60,000 all of your family's child benefit is taken away. The marginal tax rates on dividend income in the £50,000-£60,000 tax bracket are as follows:

Children	Marginal Tax Rate on Dividends
1	43%
2	51%
3	58%
4	65%

Plus 7% for each additional child.

Example

Fikile is the highest earner in a household claiming child benefit of £2,545 for three children. She runs a successful cleaning company and normally pays herself a small salary and dividend totalling £75,000. This means all of her child benefit payments are taken away each year by the child benefit charge.

Because of the uncertain economic outlook, she decides to pay herself total taxable income of just £50,000 this year, which means she avoids paying 32.5% tax and holds onto all of her child benefit for a change.

Next year she's much more confident again and decides to pay herself her usual £75,000 plus an additional £25,000 to make up for this year's shortfall. She will then have total taxable income of £100,000.

All of the additional £25,000 will be taxed at 32.5%, as is usually the case, and because she keeps her income below £100,000 next year she gets to hold onto all of her income tax personal allowance.

By being cautious this year Fikile enjoys an additional bonus of £2,545 by avoiding the child benefit charge. In fact, Fikile should consider paying herself like this in normal times as well, to preserve her child benefit every second year.

High Income Earners

Those company owners who normally pay themselves more than £125,000 per year currently enjoy no income tax personal allowance.

If you are concerned about the current economic outlook you could consider reducing your income to at least £100,000 this year to preserve your income tax personal allowance.

Catch-up dividends can then be paid in future tax years. This may actually save you tax even if the catch-up dividends take you over the £150,000 threshold where dividends are taxed at 38.1%.

This is because holding onto your income tax personal allowance can be better than avoiding the 38.1% additional rate.

Example

Sam owns a successful chain of gyms. He was planning on taking a salary of £9,500 and a dividend of £140,500 this year. His total taxable income would be £150,000, so he would avoid paying the 38.1% additional rate of tax. He has been withdrawing exactly £150,000 for several years now.

With this much income he does, however, lose all of his income tax personal allowance every year. His total income tax bill would be £40,413 this year. Over two tax years his total tax bill would be £80,826 (assuming tax rates stayed the same for simplicity).

Sam could instead consider withdrawing £100,000 this year and £200,000 next year – the same total income but split differently. If he does this his total tax bills will be £18,913 and £59,463 respectively: a total tax bill of £78,376.

Sam saves £2,450 by following this strategy. Next year he has to pay income tax of 38.1% on an extra £50,000 of dividend income: £19,050. However, this year his taxable income falls by £50,000 to £100,000, so his income tax personal allowance is fully retained. He would have paid 53.5% tax on the first £25,000 of that income and 32.5% on the final £25,000 – a total of £21,500. The difference is £2,450 (£21,500 - £19,050).

Like Fikile in the earlier example, this type of tax planning would work well in normal times as well.

Chapter 4

Company Directors: Borrowing and Lending

Borrowing from Your Company – Directors Loans

If your company does not have sufficient distributable profits to declare dividends, one option is to pay yourself a higher salary.

The problem with salaries, however, is the high national insurance cost. Any salary that exceeds £9,500 is subject to both employee's national insurance at 12% and employer's national insurance at 13.8%, unless the company has some of its £4,000 national insurance employment allowance remaining (or the director is over state pension age).

One alternative is to take a loan from your company.

With the exception of loans for under £10,000 these do generally have to be approved by the company's shareholders.

The attractiveness of taking a loan from your company is limited by two potential tax charges:

- a 32.5% tax paid by the *company* (the section 455 charge)
- a benefit-in-kind charge paid by the *director*

The Section 455 Charge

If a close company lends money to a participator (generally speaking a shareholder) *the company* will have to pay a temporary tax charge of 32.5% on the loan. This is known as the section 455 charge. So a loan for £50,000 to a director could attract a temporary tax charge of £16,250.

The tax charge does not have to be paid if the loan is repaid within nine months after the end of the company's financial year. This is the normal due date for the company's corporation tax.

This means that short-term loans to directors do not attract any company tax charge. For longer loans it is vital to make sure that the company has sufficient funds to pay the section 455 charge when it falls due.

However, the key point is that the section 455 charge will be refunded after the loan is repaid.

Unfortunately from a cashflow perspective, the company will only be repaid 9 months after the end of the accounting period in which the loan is repaid.

Benefit-in-kind Charge

If it's an interest-free loan or if the interest paid is less than the 'official rate', the director will have to pay an income tax benefit-in-kind charge. Fortunately this tax charge is extremely small.

The official rate of interest is currently 2.25% (from 6 April 2020), so if the interest charged on the loan is less than 2.25%, a benefit-in-kind charge is payable when you submit your tax return.

For example, if the loan is for £20,000 and no interest is charged, the director will face the following annual tax charge if he is a higher-rate taxpayer:

£20,000 loan x 2.25% x 40% tax = £180

If the director is a basic-rate taxpayer the annual tax charge will be just £90. The company will also have to pay class 1A national insurance:

£20,000 loan x 2.25% x 13.8% = £62

The benefit in kind is reduced to zero if interest at 2.25% or more is paid to the company.

Note, however, that the benefit in kind is only reduced if there is a formal obligation to pay interest to the company. For this reason it is probably advisable to have a properly drawn up loan agreement.

If you do pay interest, you will be paying the money to your own company rather than a bank. However, the company will pay corporation tax on the interest it receives and you will have to pay income tax when you eventually withdraw the money back out as a dividend.

It is generally cheaper, at present, to pay interest at the official rate, rather than take an interest-free loan. However, there isn't much difference and company owners should probably do what's easiest.

Loans for £10,000 or Less

There is no income tax benefit-in-kind charge if all of the loans to the director total £10,000 or less throughout the tax year.

It is important to understand that any sum due from the director to the company is counted as a 'loan', including goods or services that have been provided to the director but not paid for.

The section 455 corporation tax charge still applies if the loan is not repaid on time. Nevertheless, this exemption allows a director to take a loan of up to £10,000 for up to 21 months with no adverse tax consequences (£20,000 if the company is run by a couple).

This chapter contains just a brief overview of the rules for directors' loans. For a more detailed discussion please see the Taxcafe guide *Salary versus Dividends*.

Lending Money to Your Company

In the previous chapter we explained that a company director can pay themselves a salary or dividend by crediting it to their director's loan account. That way the money remains inside the company and the company is effectively borrowing money from the director.

Company owners can also lend other funds they have to their companies in times of financial hardship and in all cases the company can pay you interest.

In some cases the interest will be both a tax deductible expense for the company and tax free in the hands of the director – the best case scenario when it comes to extracting money from your company.

The interest could be tax free thanks to the 0% "starting rate band" for up to £5,000 of savings income.

There's also the savings allowance which shelters up to £1,000 of interest income from tax if you're a basic-rate taxpayer and £500 if you're a higher-rate taxpayer (additional-rate taxpayers do not benefit from the savings allowance).

The £5,000 Starting Rate Band

Not everyone can benefit from the 0% starting rate. It's designed to benefit those with very low income. Hence the £5,000 starting rate band is reduced if you have any *taxable non-savings income*.

Non-savings income includes income from employment, self-employment, pensions and rental properties. Crucially, it does not include dividend income.

For example, if in 2020/21 you have a salary of £12,500 and no other income apart from dividends, you won't have any taxable non-savings income and can receive £5,000 of tax-free interest from your company.

You may also be able to receive up to £1,000 of additional tax-free interest thanks to the savings allowance.

But if you have a salary of £12,500 and rental income of more than £5,000, your rental income will eat up all of your starting rate band, so none of your interest income will be tax-free under the 0% starting rate.

You may, however, be able to receive up to £1,000 of tax-free interest thanks to the savings allowance.

The Mechanics of Extracting Interest Income

There is no requirement for a director to charge interest on a loan account with their own company but if they do it must not exceed a reasonable commercial rate.

If the company pays more than a commercial rate the excess payment could be treated as salary income and subject to income tax and national insurance.

Interest paid to a director on their loan account will usually be an allowable expense for the company, providing the money is used for business purposes. The interest will therefore provide corporation tax relief.

Although your interest income may ultimately be tax free, the company will have to deduct 20% income tax and pay this to HMRC quarterly, using form CT61 which can be requested online.

If this results in a tax overpayment, the director can reclaim the excess through their self-assessment tax return.

Nevertheless, the additional reporting duties and payments may put some company owners off paying themselves any interest.

The company should also issue you an annual interest certificate.

This chapter contains just a brief overview of the rules for extracting interest income. For a more detailed discussion please see the Taxcafe guide *Salary versus Dividends*.

Chapter 5

Employing Your Children

With most schools and universities now closed until the start of the new academic year, there has never been a better time to employ your children in your business... at least in theory.

I say in theory because, at the time of writing, many families were in lockdown and unable to work! Hopefully this awful state of affairs will not last too long.

Sole traders, landlords and company owners can all employ their children. As long as the salaries are not excessive and can be justified by the amount of work done, they will be a tax deductible expense for the business.

(You can't just stick your children on the payroll while they sit at home on their Xbox! In one recent tax case a son's wages were disallowed because there were no time records or other evidence to justify the payments.)

The rate paid must also be commercially justified – in other words, no more than you would pay to a non-family member with the same level of experience and ability to do the job.

Apart from being a tax deductible expense for the business, the payments will, in many cases, be completely tax free in the hands of the child. A tax deduction coupled with a tax-free receipt is the best possible outcome when it comes to business tax planning.

Reporting Requirements

This is a very important consideration, especially if your business does not currently operate a PAYE scheme.

You may be required to report payments to your children to HMRC under the 'Real Time Information' system (RTI). Payments must be reported 'on or before' the point at which the payment is made.

Where the business does not already operate a PAYE scheme these requirements may lead to additional professional fees.

Employers must register for PAYE and report under RTI where at least one employee:

- Earns at or above the LEL (£6,240 in 2020/21)
- Has another job

Where at least one employee meets the above criteria, the employer must report information about payments made to all employees.

So even if your children earn less then the lower earnings limit their salary will still have to be reported to HMRC, if the business currently operates a PAYE scheme.

If you don't already have a PAYE scheme and your children are paid more than the LEL or have another job this may force you to operate a PAYE scheme.

However, if your business has no other employees it is not necessary to operate PAYE and submit RTI returns if your children do not have another job and earn less than the LEL.

Tax-Free Salaries

Children under 16

Those aged under 16 can be paid up to £12,500 in 2020/21 with no income tax or national insurance consequences.

Children aged 16 to 20

Children who are 16 and over have to pay 12% employee's national insurance on income over £9,500. However, there is no *employer's* national insurance payable as long as their income is below £50,000.

This means your son or daughter can be paid £9,500 completely tax free and up to £12,500 with a total tax charge of just £360.

Children 21 and Over

Children who are 21 and over can receive a completely tax-free salary of up to £8,788.

Employer's national insurance is payable on salaries over £8,788 at the rate of 13.8%. However, if the business does not use up its £4,000 national insurance allowance paying other employees, a salary of up to £9,500 can be paid completely tax free.

Bigger Salaries

In most cases the above tax-free salaries will comfortably cover part-time work done by your children at a commercially justifiable rate.

Where a bigger salary is justified additional tax savings may be achieved if your own marginal tax rate is higher than that of your child.

In most cases what you want to avoid is paying your child a salary that is subject to income tax (at 20%), employee's national insurance (at 12%) and employer's national insurance (at 13.8%).

This is especially the case where you yourself expect to be a basic-rate taxpayer this year with a marginal tax rate of just 20% (landlords), 29% (sole traders) or 25% (the combined corporation tax and income tax rate on dividend income).

Restrictions on Work and Hours

It is important to take note of the restrictions placed on the hours and types of work that children can do because this will affect how much you can pay them.

Children are of compulsory school age up to the last Friday in June in the academic year of their 16th birthday. After this they are at the 'mandatory school leaving age' and can apply for a national insurance number and work full time.

Until that time there are restrictions on the hours and types of work that can be carried out. For starters, it is generally illegal to employ children under 13 in any capacity (unless they're involved in TV or modelling).

Other children must not work:

- Without an employment permit if local byelaws require it
- In factories or on industrial sites
- During school hours
- Before 7.00 am or after 7.00 pm
- For more than 1 hour before school (local byelaws permitting)
- For more than 4 hours without taking a 1 hour break
- In occupations prohibited by byelaws/legislation (e.g. pubs)
- If the work will harm their health, well-being or education
- Without having a 2 week break during the school holidays in each calendar year

More Restrictions on Hours Worked

During term time children can work for no more than 12 hours per week including a maximum of:

- 2 hours on school days and Sundays
- 5 hours on Saturdays for 13 to 14 year olds; 8 hours for 15 to 16 year olds

During school holidays 13 to 14 year olds may work a maximum of 25 hours per week. This includes a maximum of:

- 5 hours on weekdays and Saturdays
- 2 hours on Sunday

During school holidays 15 to 16 year olds may work a maximum of 35 hours per week. This includes a maximum of:

- 8 hours on weekdays and Saturdays
- 2 hours on Sunday

Minimum Wages

A salary paid to a child must be justified by the amount of work which they actually do in your business. In other words, you cannot pay them too much.

However, it's also important to not pay them too little. If your child is below the compulsory school leaving age the national minimum wage does not apply. The national minimum wage applies to employees aged 16 to 24 and the living wage applies to those aged 25 and over.

From 1 April 2020 the hourly rates are as follows:

- £8.72   Living wage, 25 and over
- £8.20   21-24
- £6.45   18-20
- £4.55   16-17 if above school leaving age
- £4.15   apprentice rate

There is also an exemption for relatives living in the employer's household. Hence, these compulsory wage rates will often not apply to your own children, although they may still be a good yardstick to use when setting the salary level for younger children with no particular business skills. Where the child has some experience, or the role requires some skill, a higher rate will often be justified.

Chapter 6

Capital Allowances

The Annual Investment Allowance (AIA)

The annual investment allowance lets businesses claim an immediate 100% tax deduction when they buy machinery, furniture, fixtures, fittings, computers and other equipment used in a business.

In 2016 the annual investment allowance was fixed permanently at £200,000. However, in the October 2018 Budget the limit was increased to £1 million per year for two years from 1 January 2019 to 31 December 2020.

In the current climate many businesses will be holding back on their investment spending and will be unwilling or unable to take advantage of the big increase in the annual investment allowance before it is reduced again in December 2020.

It's possible that it will be kept at £1 million to help encourage business investment but we have no idea whether this will actually happen.

It's important to note that transitional rules apply to accounting periods spanning 31 December 2020 which severely restrict the AIA available on expenditure incurred in early 2021.

Example
Theresa Ltd is a company which draws up accounts to 31 March each year. For the year ending 31 March 2021 transitional rules apply to give the company a maximum Annual Investment Allowance of:

£1m x 275/365	*£753,425*
£200,000 x 90/365	*£49,315*
Total	*£802,740*

An additional rule applies to expenditure incurred after 31 December 2020. The maximum amount that can be claimed for spending between 1st January and 31 March 2021 would be £49,315.

The company's annual investment allowance for the year as a whole is £802,740. However, only £49,315 of this spending can take place between 1 January and 31 March 2021.

If the company spends, say, £200,000 between 1 January and 31 March 2021, £150,685 of this spending (£200,000 - £49,315) may only qualify for much stingier writing down allowances at 6% or 18% per year.

If the company wants to invest more than £49,315 during the current financial year it should try to ensure all the additional spending takes place before 31 December 2020.

Alternatively, the company could consider postponing some of its spending until after 31 March 2021 when it will have a fresh annual investment allowance of £200,000.

Electric Cars

For most small company owners a company car is not very tax efficient. The company can only claim a very small capital allowance each year and the director will have a large taxable benefit in kind.

Electric cars are an exception. This year, companies can claim a 100% first-year allowance for new and unused cars with CO2 emissions of 50g/km or less.

This means the company can claim the whole cost of the car as a tax deductible business expense.

Electric cars also have very low benefit-in kind charges. The taxable percentage for zero-emission cars (electric cars) is 0% this year and will rise to 1% in 2021/22 and 2% in 2022/23 and will then stay frozen for 2023/24 and 2024/25.

For cars with emissions of 1-50g/km the taxable percentage varies from 0% to 14% depending on the electric range in miles of the vehicle and the date the car is registered. Again, the taxable percentages for 2022/23 will also apply in 2023/24 and 2024/25.

If your company provides electricity to charge a fully electric company car there is no benefit in kind charge, regardless of the level of private mileage you do or where the car is charged.

The company can also pay for a charging point at your home for a fully electric car without a taxable benefit arising.

If you pay for electricity personally but use a fully electric company car for business travel, a new advisory fuel rate of 4p per mile can be used to reimburse you tax free for business mileage.

In terms of saving tax, an electric car is pretty much as good as it gets. The cost is a fully tax deductible expense for the company and the benefit is currently tax free in the hands of the director (and only lightly taxed in future tax years).

Although electric cars are very tax efficient, in the current climate many business owners may be unwilling to invest in them.

The 100% first year allowance was initially due to be taken away on 31 March 2021. Fortunately for those who won't be looking at new cars this year, the Government has announced that the 100% first year allowance has been extended until 31 March 2025.

So there's no hurry to go out and by a fully electric car before 31 March 2021.

Note, however, that from 1 April 2021 the emission thresholds for capital allowances will be as follows:

- Over 50g/km   6% per year
- 1-50g/km   18% per year
- Zero   100%

In other words, if you buy a car with CO_2 emissions of 1-50g/km before 1 April 2021 it will qualify for a 100% first year allowance. If you buy the car after this date you will only be entitled to a writing down allowance of 18% per year.

Chapter 7

Working from Home

Introduction

With most of the country having been told to stay at home the next question is: what sort of tax relief can you claim when you work from home?

In the first section we'll take a look at the position for unincorporated business owners and later on in the chapter we'll examine the position of company directors.

Landlords, Sole Traders and Partners

Working from home means you can claim part of your household costs for tax purposes.

Even in normal times almost everyone in business can make some claim for 'use of home'. We don't know any business owner who doesn't at least take some paperwork home or make business calls from home.

Many people think they can't claim because they're already claiming for an office, a shop, or other business premises. Not true!

Claims should be based on the proportionate use of the property for business. The main factors to consider are *time* and *space*: how much space is set aside for business use and how much time is spent on business.

During the current tax year, with so many people working from home more than usual, the time element is likely to be greater than normal.

There are many possible methods for calculating the business proportion. In practice, the most popular method is to simply take the number of rooms used for business as a proportion of the total number of rooms in the house. Hallways, bathrooms and kitchens are excluded from the calculation.

Example

Willie is a graphic designer and uses a room in his house as his office. The house also has two bedrooms, a living room, a dining room, two bathrooms and a kitchen.

We can ignore the bathrooms and the kitchen, so this leaves five rooms for the purpose of our calculation, meaning that Willie can claim one fifth of his household costs.

So, if Willie's annual household costs amount to £10,000 and he uses the office room exclusively for business, this entitles him to claim a tax deduction of £2,000.

Note in this example we're assuming Willie works full time from home for the whole tax year. If this is not the case he will have to reduce his claim (see below).

What Expenses Can Be Claimed?

A self-employed person working from home is entitled to claim a proportion of most household costs, including:

- Mortgage interest or rent
- Council tax
- Water rates
- Repairs and maintenance
- Building and contents insurance
- Electricity
- Gas, oil or other heating costs
- Cleaning

A proportion of general repairs and maintenance costs relating to the whole property, such as roof repairs or gas maintenance costs may be claimed.

Costs which are specific to an area used for work may be claimed in full – subject to any reduction required for partial private use of that area.

Redecorating a study used for work would be an allowable cost, for example. The flipside of this is that any costs specific to a wholly non-work area may not be claimed at all.

Capital allowances may also be claimed on any furniture and equipment used for business, with immediate 100% relief usually available thanks to the annual investment allowance, subject to a reduction for any private use.

Floor Space Instead of Rooms

What if Willie's design work requires a lot of space and the room he uses is actually the largest in the house?

In this case, it would be better if Willie did his calculation based on floor space, as this would produce a greater deduction for him.

Wasted Space

Let's suppose that Willie never uses his dining room. The room's mere existence means he is claiming just one fifth of his household costs. Arguably, if the room is never used, he might justifiably claim a quarter instead.

Better still, Willie should start using the dining room for business. Then he could claim up to two fifths of his household costs (depending on how much he uses the room).

Using a room for business can take many forms – completing paperwork, taking business calls, meeting customers, storing files or other business items – even just sitting there thinking about your business.

Reduce Your Claim and Save Capital Gains Tax

When there is some private use of a room used for business, you will need to restrict your home office claim.

For example, let's say once a week, Willie usually has some friends round for a game of poker and they use his office. They play for about four hours each week. Willie works in his office for 46 hours a week on average, so his business use amounts to 46/50ths, or 92%.

With total annual household costs of £10,000 and five rooms to be taken into account, this means Willie may now claim a deduction of £1,840 (£10,000 x 1/5 x 92%).

"Why don't they play cards in the dining room?" you may ask. One possible reason is that Willie wants to protect his Capital Gains Tax (CGT) exemption.

The CGT exemption which you usually get when you sell your home is restricted if part of the house has been used exclusively for business.

Fortunately, as long as there is some private use of each room in the house, no matter how small, your CGT relief is safe.

(Willie and his friends probably can't play poker at the moment but, as long as there is some private use of his office some of the time, his CGT exemption remains safe.)

Time-Based Claims

For smaller properties, looking at floor space or number of rooms may be unsuitable and it will often make more sense to make claims on a time basis instead.

Example
Donna is a self-employed web designer. She works at home in her small one bedroom flat. Because her flat is so small, Donna is effectively using the whole flat for business when she is working. Conversely, of course, when she isn't working, she is using the whole flat privately.

In this case, we could use what I call the 'work, rest and play' principle - assuming Donna spends an equal amount of time on each, she should claim one third of her household costs.

Many self-employed people work more than a third of the time, so a greater claim will sometimes be justified.

Since HMRC staff are not self-employed, it may be wise to retain some evidence of your actual working hours in order to convince them of this!

Part-Timers

Those who generally work from home only part of the time, such as at evenings and weekends, have to reduce their claim accordingly.

The methods for allocating household costs described above remain available, but a further reduction in the claim must be applied to reflect the part-time nature of the business use of part of the home.

Establishing this reduction needs to be considered on a case by case basis. The key watchword to remember is: be reasonable!

Let's say, for example, that you normally use your dining room for business purposes around 20 hours each week, but the room is also used privately (for meals, the children doing their homework, etc) around 30 hours each week. So, 40% of the room's total usage is business use.

Let's also say that there are five other rooms which we need to take into account (excluding hallways, bathrooms and kitchen, as usual) and your total annual household costs are £10,000.

In this case, it would seem reasonable for you to normally claim £667 (£10,000 x 1/6 x 40%) in respect of business use of your home.

But what if, because of the coronavirus lockdown, during the current tax year you have used the dining room for business purposes for 30 hours per week on average and 20 hours per week privately.

In this case, it would seem reasonable for you to claim £1,000 (£10,000 x 1/6 x 60%) in respect of business use of your home this year.

As your dining room is used quite extensively (50 hours per week in total), it does not seem necessary, in this case, to look at 'fixed' costs like council tax and mortgage interest, differently to 'variable' costs like electricity.

Let's look at another example, however.

Example

Freema is a self-employed freelance consultant and she normally does some work at home amounting to around three hours per week on average.

Based on the usual test, her flat has three rooms to be taken into account, including the spare bedroom which she only uses for work and for the occasional guest. She has very few guests, so her business use of the spare room amounts to 90% of the room's total usage.

Freema's total annual household costs amount to £10,000.

If we used our usual formula, this would produce a claim of £3,000 (£10,000 x 1/3 x 90%).

However, taking a reasonable view, we see that this amounts to a rather ridiculous and unsustainable claim of over £19 per hour of business use.

Hence, in this case, it seems reasonable to apply HMRC's approach, whereby 'fixed' costs are allocated on the basis of how much time the room is actually used for business as a proportion of how much time the room is available for use.

Let's say that Freema has £8,000 of 'fixed' costs and £2,000 of variable costs. There are 168 hours in a week, but it is reasonable to assume that a room is only available for use 16 hours per day, or 112 hours per week. Freema's tax deduction is therefore calculated as follows:

Fixed costs:	*£8,000 x 1/3 x 3/112*	*£71*
Variable costs:	*£2,000 x 1/3 x 90%*	*£600*
Total claim:		*£671*

This is a much more reasonable and sensible claim in Freema's case.

Example Revisited

Let's say during the current tax year Freema is forced to work at home for 10 hours per week on average. Her tax deduction is therefore calculated as follows

Fixed costs:	*£8,000 x 1/3 x 10/112*	*£238*
Variable costs:	*£2,000 x 1/3 x 90%*	*£600*
Total claim:		*£838*

For these types of calculations, fixed costs would include:

- Mortgage interest or rent
- Council tax
- Water rates (but not if the supply is metered)
- Building and contents insurance

Minimal Use

For cases where there is only minimal business use of the home, HMRC's instructions suggest that claims of up to £2 a week (or £104 a year) will be acceptable, although some actual business use of the home is required, even if only very small. It isn't much, but it saves the effort of doing any more complex calculations.

It is worth noting that the £2 per week rate has been included in HMRC's manuals relating to self-employed business income for some time. Meanwhile, the rate allowed to employees working from home has been increased to £6 per week (or £312 a year) and some commentators believe it is reasonable to assume HMRC will now allow this same rate for self-employed business owners rather than the £2 per week shown in the business income manual. Sadly, the position here is not entirely clear!

Flat Rate Deductions

A system of flat rate deductions for business use of your home is also available for trading businesses.

The flat rate deductions are an alternative method which is available instead of the proportionate calculation discussed above.

The amount of the deduction is calculated on a monthly basis according to the number of hours spent wholly and exclusively working on business matters. The rates applying are:

Hours worked in the month	Deduction allowed for the month
25 to 50	£10
51 to 100	£18
101 or more	£26

Example

Clara is a self-employed person who draws up accounts to 31ˢᵗ March each year and normally works at home for 30 hours per month. This means she can normally claim a tax deduction of £120 per year (12 months x £10).

However, during the current tax year she works at home for at least 101 hours per month for four months. This means she can claim a tax deduction of:

8 months at £10 per month	*£80*
4 months at £26 per month	*£104*

Her total tax deduction is £184.

The flat rate doesn't include telephone or internet expenses. The taxpayer can still claim the business proportion of these costs by working out the actual costs.

The flat rate deductions are not exactly generous and anyone who feels that it is not worthwhile performing complex calculations to arrive at a suitable proportion of household expenses can still claim the simple deduction of £2 per week described above.

In our last example, Clara could have claimed a 'use of home' deduction of £104 for the year ending 31ˢᵗ March 2021 without having to carry out **any** calculations (some people would argue she could claim £312 in fact: for the reasons explained above).

She would almost certainly be better off carrying out a proper calculation and claiming a suitable proportion of her actual household running costs.

Company Directors

Directors and other employees may only claim the specific additional costs of working from home – generally just heating and lighting. Where it is impractical to calculate the exact costs, a claim of £6 per week is permitted.

They must also be required to work from home: simply choosing to do so is not enough. If you run your company from home and have no other business premises, this is pretty obvious. In other cases, you will need to demonstrate a genuine need to carry out your duties at home and may also need to stipulate a requirement to do so in your employment contract.

However, during the current lockdown, it is clear that many company directors are required to work from home under Government guidelines. Hence, at present, we would argue there is no need for this to be included in an employment contract and most small company directors should be able to claim a deduction for working from home – either at £6 per week or a greater amount if detailed calculations support it. For example, if a director has a house with four rooms (excluding kitchen, bathroom and hallways as usual), variable household costs of £200 per month, and has to use one room exclusively for work because of the lockdown, they may claim a deduction of £50 (£200 x 1/4) per month during the lockdown period.

(Short-term exclusive use should not affect your CGT exemption on the property, but long-term exclusive use should be avoided.)

In order to get tax relief, extra salary over and above the personal allowance will be required. This will lead to additional National Insurance costs. In some cases, this can be avoided by having the company reimburse the costs instead.

A better alternative in many cases is for the company to rent space at the director's house. A suitable proportion of all household costs can be deducted from the rent received and no National Insurance will be due. The company will also be able to claim Corporation Tax relief for the rent paid. Furthermore, by granting the company a 'non-exclusive licence to occupy' the relevant space, and maintaining some private use outside working hours, any restriction in CGT relief on your home can be avoided.

Chapter 8

Pension Contributions

Preserving Your Cash

Pensions are a wonderful way to save for your retirement and in many cases a much more powerful tax shelter than ISAs.

If you are a higher-rate taxpayer while you are making contributions and a basic-rate taxpayer when you retire (most retirees are basic-rate taxpayers), you could end up with at least 41.67% more income by saving through a pension instead of an ISA (see the Taxcafe guide *Pension Magic* for more information).

However, the problem with pensions is your money is locked up until you reach age 55 (rising to 57 in 2028) and there are other restrictions on the amount of money you can withdraw without penalty.

For this reason anyone concerned about their cash position in the current climate should consider reducing or halting their pension contributions for a period.

Although this may result in a higher tax bill during the current tax year, most people will be able to completely reverse this tax increase by making bigger contributions in future tax years.

At present most individuals can make pension contributions of up to £40,000 per year and carry forward any unused allowance from the three previous tax years. So if you don't make any pension contributions during the current tax year, you will be able to make a contribution of at least £80,000 next year.

High Income Earners

Note, some high earners may not be able to make a pension contribution of £40,000 per year if they are subject to the tapered annual allowance.

Fortunately, following an announcement in the March 2020 Budget, the pension taper now only kicks in at much higher income levels than previously.

If your 'threshold income' is £200,000 or less you are completely exempt from tapering and can make pension contributions just like anyone else.

Your threshold income is, broadly speaking, your total taxable income minus any pension contributions you have made *personally*. Contributions by your employer are ignored.

Protecting Higher-Rate Tax Relief

Another reason why it may be a good idea to reduce or postpone your pension contributions is to protect your higher-rate tax relief if you expect your income to fall during the current tax year

For the current 2020/21 tax year if your taxable income is more than £50,000 you can enjoy higher-rate tax relief on your pension contributions. If your income is less than £50,000 all you will get is basic-rate tax relief.

Example
Sandy is a sole trader who expects to have a pre-tax profit of £40,000 this year, which is much lower than normal. If he invests £4,000 in his pension the taxman will also add £1,000 of basic-rate relief to his pension pot. But because Sandy is not a higher-rate taxpayer he will not enjoy any higher-rate tax relief.

Let's say next year the higher-rate threshold is £50,000 again and Sandy expects to have pre-tax profits of £60,000. If he invests £4,000 in his pension the taxman will add £1,000 of basic-rate relief, resulting in a gross pension contribution of £5,000.

Because Sandy is now a higher-rate taxpayer he can also claim higher-rate tax relief when he submits his tax return. This is found by multiplying his gross pension contribution by 20%:

$$£5,000 \times 20\% = £1,000$$

What this example shows is that higher-rate taxpayers enjoy twice as much tax relief on their pension contributions as basic-rate taxpayers.

If Sandy postpones making pension contributions this year (with only basic-rate tax relief available), he can catch up by making an additional gross contribution of £5,000 next year. He will enjoy full higher-rate tax relief on this additional contribution.

An added benefit of postponing his pension contribution is that, if Sandy is the highest earner in a household claiming child benefit, he will completely avoid the child benefit charge next year. This is because his £10,000 gross pension contribution will reduce his adjusted net income from £60,000 to £50,000.

It's important to point out that you can only enjoy higher-rate tax relief on your pension contributions if you have enough income taxed at 40%.

The maximum amount you can contribute in any one year with full higher-rate tax relief is:

Your taxable income <u>minus</u> the higher-rate threshold

For example, if your taxable income is £60,000 and the higher-rate threshold is £50,000 the maximum contribution you can make with full higher-rate tax relief is £10,000. This is your maximum *gross* pension contribution (which includes the taxman's top up). Multiply this number by 0.8 to obtain the maximum amount you invest personally: £8,000.

Sandy in the above example will be claiming the maximum higher-rate tax relief when he makes his catch-up contribution next year. If his contributions were any larger he would only enjoy basic-rate tax relief on the excess.

If you're making bigger than normal catch-up contributions its important to check that you will receive higher-rate tax relief on the whole amount.

Note, the higher-rate threshold is £43,430 in Scotland, which means anyone with taxable income of more than £43,430 can enjoy higher-rate tax relief.

Fear of Missing Out

Many financial advisors would probably argue that, with the stock market having fallen by over 30% in recent months, now is the wrong time to halt your pension contributions. Instead you should be drip feeding money into the stock market to take advantage of some of the "bargains" on offer.

They may be right or they may be wrong. We have now idea where the stock market is heading in the months of years ahead.

It's important to remember that there are other ways to save and invest without locking up your money. For example, if you have not already used up your £20,000 ISA allowance you could stick your retirement savings in an ISA, enjoy tax-free income and capital gains, and later on put the money into your pension with full tax relief.

However, most financial advisers would agree that you should not be investing money in risky assets if you think you may need the money to cover your living costs in the short term.

Regular Salaried Employees

Not everyone should consider reducing or halting their pension contributions.

If you belong to a workplace pension scheme to which your employer is also contributing, halting your own contributions could prove costly: you will also lose out on the contribution your employer is making, which could be significantly larger than your own.

The main focus of this chapter is discretionary pension contributions, not the compulsory minimum contributions required by those who are automatically enrolled into their employers' pension schemes.

Employees can opt out of their employers' workplace pension schemes at any time, although most would advise against this.

Company Owners

Company owners often get their companies to make pension contributions on their behalf because this is slightly more tax efficient than making them personally.

Furthermore, many company owners only pay themselves a small salary and can therefore only make a small pension contribution personally. Contributions made by you personally must not exceed your annual earnings, typically your salary.

Pension contributions made by a company are not restricted by the level of the director's earnings. A company pension contribution can be a lot bigger than the director's earnings.

There are, however, other restrictions and the company may be denied corporation tax relief on any pension contribution that is viewed as 'excessive', although this is fairly rare in practice.

Pension contributions are an extremely tax efficient way to extract money from your company. When you retire you may be able to pay tax on your pension income at an effective rate of just 15%, compared with the overall tax rate of 25% or 45% you may currently be paying on your dividend income.

However, anyone concerned about their company's cash position in the current climate should consider reducing or halting their company pension contributions for a period.

Although this may result in a higher corporation tax bill for the current financial year, it should be possible to completely reverse this tax increase by making bigger contributions in future years.

Reducing pension contributions may also make it easier to pay yourself dividend income in the near future, rather than having to pay yourself a much more heavily taxed salary or resort to borrowing money from your company.

As we saw in Chapter 3, a company must have sufficient distributable profits to pay dividends. Pension contributions *reduce* a company's taxable profit, which means there will be less after-tax profit to distribute as dividends.

Tapping Your Pension Pot in an Emergency

Some people who are 55 or older may be thinking about tapping their pension pots for the first time, for example those whose incomes have fallen dramatically during the coronavirus pandemic.

This is arguably the worst thing you could do if your pension savings are invested in the stock market because you could end up realising large losses on your investments.

That aside, those who do decide to withdraw money from their pensions can use flexi-access drawdown to withdraw 25% of their savings as a tax-free lump sum. The remaining savings can then be placed into drawdown where they can continue to grow tax free.

You can also resume making annual pension contributions of up to £40,000 per year when your financial position improves.

What you want to avoid at all costs is withdrawing anything more than your tax-free lump sum. As soon as you start withdrawing *taxable income* you are subject to the money purchase annual allowance which limits your pension contribution to just £4,000 per year forever.

If you are subject to the money purchase annual allowance you also cannot carry forward any unused allowance from previous tax years.

Chapter 9

ISAs, VCTs and Mortgages

Introduction

Some investments are much more liquid than others, which means you can get your hands on your money quickly if you need it.

We've already discussed in the previous chapter why it may be a good idea to reduce or halt your pension contributions this year if you are worried about your cash position. This is because pension savings are placed in a locked box until you're 55 and there are other restrictions when you start withdrawing money.

The general rule is the more generous the tax shelter, the more difficult it is to get your hands on your money. So this year many individuals may have to consider sacrificing tax savings in favour of retaining access to their cash.

Traditional ISAs

Instant access cash ISAs are arguably the most liquid type of tax shelter because you can generally get hold of your money at any time.

Some cash ISAs do, however, have a 120 day notice period and don't offer much more interest than instant access accounts.

Fixed-rate ISAs offer a fixed rate for between one and five years and there will be a penalty if you withdraw any money before the end of the term.

The investments in a stocks and shares ISA can be liquidated at any time and the cash can be paid out, although this may not be very appealing if your investments are all showing a loss at present!

Lifetime ISAs

Those aged 18 to 39 can open a Lifetime ISA which can be used to save for a first home or for retirement.

Any money you put in (up to £4,000 per year) will receive a 25% Government bonus. So if you put in £4,000, the Government will add £1,000.

Contributions to a Lifetime ISA fall within the overall £20,000 ISA subscription limit. In other words, if you invest £4,000 in your Lifetime ISA you can invest another £16,000 in a traditional ISA.

Unlike a pension, your savings are not locked up inside a Lifetime ISA and can be accessed in a financial emergency.

However, if you withdraw money before reaching age 60, for any reason other than to buy your first home, there will be a 25% early withdrawal charge. This will claw back all of the Government bonus, plus an additional 6.25% of the amount you invested.

For example, if you invest £1,000, the Government will add £250, giving you total savings of £1,250. If you then decide to withdraw the money, the 25% penalty will be £312.50, leaving you with £937.50. Thus you will lose the Government bonus plus an extra £62.50 (6.25%) out of the amount you originally invested.

Junior ISAs

Junior ISAs are available for minors. Parents, grandparents and others can invest up to £9,000 this year, a big increase over last year.

However, no withdrawals are permitted before the child is 18 years old. For this reason grandparents, in particular, should think twice about tying up money in these accounts. It may be better to hold onto the cash in case the parents need it in the months ahead and make bigger catch-up contributions later on.

Venture Capital Trusts

VCTs are generous tax shelters, providing 30% up front income tax relief and tax-free dividends and capital gains.

However, your money is effectively locked away for at least five years. So VCTs are not the best investment in the current climate for anyone worried about their personal cash position.

The share prices of some VCTs have fallen by over 50% during the current turmoil, which shows just how risky these investments can be.

Some may argue that now would be a good time for the brave to invest but you can also invest in ordinary small company funds via an ISA. You'll lose out on the 30% up front tax relief but your money will not be tied up.

Reducing Your Mortgage

Paying down your mortgage can be very tax efficient.

This is because not paying interest on the money you borrow is almost always much better than earning interest on the money you save.

If paying off £10,000 of debt means you don't have to pay 3% interest on that debt, you have effectively earned 3% tax free. That's much better than earning, say, 1% from a savings account.

However, in the current climate reducing your mortgage may not be a very good idea if it means you will no longer be able to get your hands on the cash. It may be better to accept a smaller return by keeping your money in a savings account.

Chapter 10

Tax Years and Accounting Dates

Accounting Dates

In the next few chapters, we are going to look at some immediate cashflow and longer term planning issues for unincorporated businesses (sole traders, partnerships, and landlords operating as individuals).

Before we do that, we need to look at how your own accounting period relates to the tax year, as this will affect the cashflow impact of your actions for tax purposes.

The date on which your accounting period ends is known as your 'accounting date' or your 'year-end' date. Usually, most businesses stick with the same accounting date each year, so all their accounting periods are of twelve months' duration.

However, the beginning and end of a business's life will usually lead to accounting periods of different lengths, as will any change to your accounting date: an option which we will explore in Chapter 12.

Keeping it Simple

Individual landlords are required to report their property income for the tax year ending on 5th April each year, so this is effectively their accounting date in the vast majority of cases.

Many other businesses also use the tax year end on 5th April for their accounting date. This keeps life simple (although not always optimal).

For these businesses it is easy to understand how your profits are taxed (or losses relieved). Your profit for the year to 5th April 2020 is the basis for your 2019/20 tax bill; your profit for the year ending 5th April 2021 is the basis for your 2020/21 tax bill.

A Fair Approximation

The 31st March is another popular year end for businesses. This is treated as a fair approximation to using the tax year end. Hence, the year ended 31st March 2020 forms the basis of your 2019/20 tax bill; the year ended 31st March 2021 forms the basis of your 2020/21 tax bill.

While there is generally little difference between a 31st March or 5th April year end, it remains important to be aware of *your* year end when undertaking any year-end tax planning. For example, if you have a 31st March year end, expenditure incurred on 1st April will only be allowed in the following tax year.

More Complex – but More Planning Opportunities

Many other businesses use different accounting dates. Generally, once the business has been in existence for a few years, the results for each accounting period form the basis for your tax bill for the tax year in which the accounting period ends. Here are a few examples:

Year ended 30th April 2020:	taxed in 2020/21
Year ended 30th June 2020:	taxed in 2020/21
Year ended 31st December 2020:	taxed in 2020/21
Year ended 30th April 2021:	taxed in 2021/22
Year ended 30th June 2021:	taxed in 2021/22

Accounting dates early in the tax year are often favoured by tax advisers as, not only is the tax on profits significantly deferred, but there is also more time to carry out tax planning and take account of subsequent events. For example, subject to the payments on account system (see Chapter 11), the tax on profits for the year ending 30th April 2020 is not due until 31st January 2022, by which time the business owner will have had ample opportunity to take into account their results for the year ending 30th April 2021 (e.g. these may give rise to a loss which could be carried back – see Chapter 36).

Generally speaking, these early accounting dates also allow more time to put other planning steps in place, such as making pension contributions (contributions made by 5th April 2021 would reduce the tax on profits for the year ending 30th April 2020), although that may be less relevant at present.

Exceptions

There are three important exceptions to the above rules that we need to bear in mind. Different rules apply to businesses not using a 31st March or 5th April year end:

- During the first three tax years of the business's life (see below)
- For the tax year in which the business ceases, including cases where a business is transferred to a company, aka 'incorporation' (see Chapter 32)
- When you change your accounting date: such changes represent a major tax planning opportunity, so we will examine this issue in detail in Chapter 12

Early Years

Special rules apply to new trading businesses in their first three tax years. During this period, the business owner can draw up accounts for any periods they wish, although most business owners pick a year end date and stick to it.

These rules may seem rather complicated but please bear with me, as they provide huge planning opportunities for new trading businesses suffering significant reductions in profits during the Coronavirus Crisis. We will start to look at those planning opportunities in this chapter and also return to look at them again in Chapter 12.

In applying the rules set out below, 31st March may, as usual, be taken as a reasonable approximation for 5th April.

Year 1
The business is taxed on its results for the period from date of commencement to the following 5th April.

Year 2
If the business has an accounting date falling in the tax year, which is at least twelve months after the date of commencement, the business is taxed on its results for the twelve months ending on that date. If there is more than one accounting date that would meet this criterion, the business is taxed on its results for the twelve months ending on the latest such date.

If one or more accounting periods end during the tax year, but all of them end within less than twelve months from the date of commencement, the business is taxed on its results for its first twelve months of trading.

If no accounting period ends during the tax year, the business is taxed on its results for the tax year.

Year 3
If one or more accounting periods end during the tax year, the business is taxed on its results for the twelve months ending on the latest accounting date.

If no accounting period ends during the tax year, the business is taxed on its results for the twelve months following the end of whatever period it was taxed on in Year 2.

Example Part 1
Angela commenced trading on 1st September 2019. For the first six months, she made a profit of £2,000 per month. From March to June 2020, she made a loss of £1,000 per month; then from July to September, she returned to a profit of £2,000 per month, rising to £3,000 per month from October 2020 onwards.

She decides to draw up accounts to 31st March each year, meaning her taxable profits for her first three tax years of trading will be:

2019/20

September 2019 to February 2020 – £2,000 x 6	*£12,000*
March 2020	*(£1,000)*

Taxable profit for the year	*£11,000*

2020/21

April to June 2020 – (£1,000) x 3	*(£3,000)*
July to September 2020 – £2,000 x 3	*£6,000*
October 2020 to March 2021 – £3,000 x 6	*£18,000*

Taxable profit for the year	*£21,000*

2021/22

April 2021 to March 2022 – £3,000 x 12	£36,000

Taxable profit for the year	£36,000
Total profits taxed over three years:	£68,000

Example Part 2

Sticking to the same facts as 'Part 1' above, let's now look what would have happened if Angela decided to draw up accounts to 30th June each year instead. Firstly, let's see what her accounts would have shown:

Ten Month Period ending 30th June 2020

September 2019 to February 2020 – £2,000 x 6	£12,000
March to June 2020 – (£1,000) x 4	(£4,000)

Profit per accounts	£8,000

Year ending 30th June 2021

July to September 2020 – £2,000 x 3	£6,000
October 2020 to June 2021 – £3,000 x 9	£27,000

Profit per accounts	£33,000

Now let's see how these profits would be taxed:

2019/20

Tax on period from commencement to 5th April 2020 (taking 31st March 2020 as a fair approximation)

10 months ending 30th June 2020: £8,000 x 7/10	£5,600

Taxable profit for the year	£5,600

2020/21

The accounting period ending during the year is of less than twelve months duration, so the business is taxed on its results for its first twelve months of trading

Ten Month Period ending 30th June 2020	£8,000
Year ending 30th June 2021	
£33,000 x 2/12	£5,500

Taxable profit for the year	£13,500

2021/22
Taxed on twelve months ending on the latest accounting date

Year ending 30th June 2021	£33,000

Taxable profit for the year	£33,000
Total profits taxed over three years:	£52,100

Example Part 3
Now let's look at what would have happened if Angela adopted 30th April as her accounting date, but did not draw up her first set of accounts until 30th April 2021. As before, we will start by looking at what her accounts would have shown:

Twenty Month Period ending 30th April 2021

September 2019 to February 2020 – £2,000 x 6	£12,000
March to June 2020 – (£1,000) x 4	(£4,000)
July to September 2020 – £2,000 x 3	£6,000
October 2020 to April 2021 – £3,000 x 7	£21,000

Profit per accounts	£35,000

Once again, we will now look at how these profits would be taxed:

2019/20
Taxed on period from commencement to 5th April 2020 (taking 31st March 2020 as a fair approximation)

Twenty Month Period ending 30th April 2021	
£35,000 x 7/20 =	£12,250

Taxable profit for the year	£12,250

2020/21
There is no accounting period ending during the year, so the business is taxed on the results for the tax year itself

Twenty Month Period ending 30th April 2021	
£35,000 x 12/20 =	£21,000

Taxable profit for the year	£21,000

2021/22
Taxed on twelve months ending on the latest accounting date

Twenty Month Period ending 30th April 2021
£35,000 x 12/20 =   £21,000

Taxable profit for the year   £21,000

Total profits taxed over three years: £54,250

As we can see, the choice of accounting date in these early years can make an enormous difference to how much profit is taxable, and when. This is particularly useful at present, during the current Coronavirus Crisis.

Overlap Profits

As Parts 2 and 3 of the example demonstrate, the 'early years' rules sometimes result in the same profits being taxed more than once, in two, or even three, different tax years. This is not necessarily a bad thing as, for businesses with rising profits, it also means the tax on higher profit levels in later periods is effectively being deferred.

Where the same profits are taxed more than once, the amounts which have been double-counted are termed 'overlap profits'. The business owner will be able to claim relief for these double-counted profits at a later date. For those with established businesses, who have overlap profits brought forward from their early years of trading, this may be a good way to save tax during the Coronavirus Crisis, so we will look at how this works in Chapters 12 and 32.

As far as the example is concerned, there were no overlap profits in Part 1; in Part 2 they amounted to £11,100 (£8,000 x 7/10 + £33,000 x 2/12); in Part 3 they amounted to £19,250 (£35,000 x 11/20), as a total of 31 months' worth of profit was taxed for the twenty month accounting period ending 30th April 2021.

Final Analysis

Which year-end accounting date will be best for Angela depends on what other taxable income she has, so we will return to this subject when we focus in more detail on tax planning with accounting dates in Chapter 12.

Chapter 11

Tax Payments and Payments on Account

To understand the cashflow implications of your tax planning, you also need to understand how tax payments work. Owners of unincorporated businesses generally pay Income Tax and National Insurance on their profits through self-assessment as follows:

31· January during the tax year:	first payment on account
31· July following the tax year:	second payment on account
31· January following the tax year:	balancing payment or repayment

However, as has been well-publicised, **the payments on account which would normally be due on 31st July 2020 do not now need to be paid and the relevant tax will be due on 31st January 2021 instead**. In effect, this means unincorporated business owners will have a larger balancing payment to make on 31st January 2021. We will look at the impact of this below.

Default Position
Payments on account under self-assessment are ***normally*** equal to half the Income Tax and Class 4 National Insurance due under self-assessment for the previous year. The critical point to note at this stage is that ***you can apply to reduce payments on account*** where you expect your final tax liability for the following year to be lower. We will examine this crucial issue further below but, in the meantime, we will stick with the default position where no such application is made.

Class 2 National Insurance and Capital Gains Tax are also paid through self-assessment but are not included within payments on account (although Capital Gains Tax on UK residential property disposals taking place after 5th April 2020 is due within 30 days of completion – see further in Chapter 41).

Example 1
Belinda is a sole trader with a small trading business. She has no other sources of income. Her taxable profits for 2018/19 were £60,000, giving rise to an Income Tax liability of £12,360 and Class 4 National

Insurance of £3,686. As a result, her payments on account in respect of 2019/20, which would **normally** have been due on 31st January and 31st July 2020, were £8,023 each.

Belinda's taxable profits for 2019/20 are £70,000, which gives her a final Income Tax liability of £15,500 and Class 4 National Insurance of £4,123. She must also pay Class 2 National Insurance of £156 for 2019/20, bringing her total liability for the year up to £19,779. Her payments on account for 2020/21 are £9,812 each.

Normal Position
To summarise, under normal circumstances, Belinda's tax payments would have been as follows (for the sake of illustration, I am ignoring any balancing payment or repayment in respect of 2018/19 which was due on 31st January 2020).

31st January 2020
First payment on account for 2019/20   £8,023

31st July 2020
Second payment on account for 2019/20   £8,023

31st January 2021
Final liability for 2019/20   £19,779
Less:
Payments on account already paid   (£16,046)

Balancing payment for 2019/20   £3,733
First payment on account for 2020/21   £9,812

Total due 31st January 2021   £13,545

31st July 2021
Second payment on account for 2020/21   £9,812

Revised Position
Following the Government announcement suspending payments due on 31st July 2020, Belinda's payments will now be as follows:

31st January 2020
First payment on account for 2019/20   £8,023

31st July 2020
No payment on account due   -

31st January 2021
Final liability for 2019/20	£19,779
Less:	
Payment on account already paid	(£8,023)

Balancing payment for 2019/20	£11,756
First payment on account for 2020/21	£9,812

Total due 31st January 2021	£21,568

31st July 2021
Second payment on account for 2020/21	£9,812

As we can see, while the deferral of the July 2020 payment on account is very welcome, the result for many businesses will be a huge tax bill on 31st January 2021.

Taxed Income

Where an unincorporated business owner has already paid tax under PAYE (on employment income or private pensions), this tax is not included in the self-assessment system and is deducted from their final self-assessment liability.

Example 2
In 2019/20 Claude had employment income of £40,000 and rental profits of £25,000 from a portfolio of residential properties (the properties are debt free so we do not need to be concerned with the restrictions on interest relief applying to residential landlords).

His total taxable income is £65,000, giving him a total Income Tax liability of £13,500 for 2019/20. However, he has already suffered deductions of £5,500 under PAYE, so his self-assessment tax liability for the year is £8,000 (£13,500 – £5,500). His payments on account in respect of 2020/21, due on 31st January and 31st July 2021, will be £4,000 each.

Payment Exceptions
Payments on account need not be made when the previous year's self-assessment liability was either:

a)   No more than £1,000, or
b)   Less than 20% of the individual's total tax for the year

Hence, for example, where an individual's self-assessment liability for 2019/20 is no more than £1,000, no payments on account in respect of 2020/21 will be due on 31st January or 31st July 2021.

Individuals in employment, or in receipt of a private pension, may apply to have self-assessment tax liabilities of up to £3,000 collected through their PAYE codes for the following tax year. This produces a considerable cashflow advantage.

The self-assessment system is also used to collect certain student loan repayments.

Reducing Payments on Account

You can apply to reduce your payments on account when you have reasonable grounds to believe your self-assessment tax liability for the following year will be less than the amounts due under the 'default position' described above. In effect, this means you can claim a reduction in your payments on account when you expect the tax due for 2019/20 will be less than the tax due for 2018/19; or the tax due for 2020/21 will be less than the tax due for 2019/20. Many owners of unincorporated businesses are likely to find themselves in this position so what, in practice, do they need to do?

The first opportunity to claim a reduction in payments on account is on your tax return. However, this is now too late for most people as far as the 2019 Tax Return, which was due for filing online by 31st January 2020, is concerned.

While the Government has now deferred payments on account which would normally be due on 31st July 2020, the ability to reduce payments on account will still be important for:

- Business owners whose taxable profits for 2019/20 have fallen significantly, meaning that the first payment on account already made in January 2020 now appears to exceed half their final tax liability
- More commonly, business owners whose taxable profits for 2020/21 are significantly lower than in 2019/20 and who therefore need to reduce their payments on account due in January and July 2021

As far as the first group are concerned, while they may not have applied to reduce their payments on account through their tax return, a later application can be made either online (if you have an online account with HMRC) or using Form SA303.

More information on applications to reduce payments on account can be found at:

www.gov.uk/understand-self-assessment-bill/payments-on-account

Form SA303 can be downloaded from:

www.gov.uk/government/publications/self-assessment-claim-to-reduce-payments-on-account-sa303

Repayment of Payments on Account made in January 2020

If you now anticipate your tax liability for 2019/20 will be reduced as a result of the Coronavirus Crisis (or indeed for any other reason), you can still claim to reduce your 2019/20 payments on account and thus obtain a refund of the amount now effectively overpaid on 31st January 2020.

Example 3.1
In January 2020, Debbie made a payment on account of £10,000 towards her 2019/20 self-assessment tax liability. This was based on her actual liability for 2018/19. At the time, she expected her 2019/20 liability to be at least £20,000, so she did not apply to reduce her payments on account.

She now realises her taxable profits for 2019/20 are likely to be drastically reduced due to losses sustained in the last month of the year. She calculates her estimated liability for 2019/20 at £11,000.

Debbie therefore applies to reduce her payments on account for 2019/20 to £5,500 each. This means she has now overpaid by £4,500 in January and can claim a suitable repayment.

Loss Carry Back Claims and Payments on Account

For most people, the impact of the Coronavirus Crisis is more likely to affect their 2020/21 tax liabilities than 2019/20. In itself this means there are no grounds for applying to reduce the payments on account due in 2020.

However, as explained in Chapter 36, a loss incurred in 2020/21 can be carried back for set off against your taxable income in 2019/20, thus reducing your 2019/20 liability and meaning, in turn, you have reasonable grounds for applying to reduce the payment on account already made in January 2020.

Example 4

Elaine runs a small cafe and bookshop and draws up accounts to 30th June each year. She was doing quite well until the Coronavirus Crisis and made profits of £50,000 in the year ended 30th June 2018 and £60,000 in the year ended 30th June 2019. Accordingly, she made a payment on account of £5,923 in January 2020, towards her tax liability for 2019/20 (as explained in Chapter 10, her 2019/20 liability is based on her profit for the year ended 30th June 2019).

Sadly, however, as she is unable to trade from mid-March 2020 onwards, she ends up incurring a loss of £25,000 for the year ended 30th June 2020. This loss falls into the 2020/21 tax year, but Elaine is able to carry it back and set it against her profits for 2019/20 (i.e. the £60,000 per her accounts to 30th June 2019). This reduces her taxable income for 2019/20 to £35,000 (£60,000 – £25,000).

Elaine now calculates her final Income Tax and Class 4 National Insurance liability for 2019/20 will be just £6,873 in total. Accordingly, she applies to reduce her payments on account for 2019/20 to £3,436 each. This means she has now overpaid by £2,487 in January and can claim a suitable repayment.

Payments on Account due in 2021

As we saw in Example 1, the self-assessment tax liabilities due on 31st January 2021 will be made up of significantly increased balancing payments for 2019/20, together with the first payment on account due for 2020/21. In effect, without any further action, most unincorporated business owners will face the prospect of paying a year's worth of tax in a single day. That year's worth of tax will be based on taxable profits for 2019/20 which, in most cases, are likely to remain at quite a high level (since the Coronavirus Crisis did not really affect most businesses until March 2020).

However, the good news is that, when completing your 2020 Tax Return, you will be able to apply to reduce your payments on account for 2020/21, in many cases to zero or to a level considerably less than the 'default position' discussed above.

At the same time, you will be able to make a provisional claim for loss relief in respect of losses carried back from 2020/21 to 2019/20, where applicable, thus also reducing the balancing payment for 2019/20. Loss relief claims are covered in more detail in Chapter 36.

Reasonable Grounds and Estimating Tax Due

You can only apply to reduce your payments on account where you have 'reasonable grounds' to expect your final tax liability for the relevant year to be less than the amounts due under the 'default position' above. Remember, in this case, we are talking about your final liability for Income Tax and Class 4 National Insurance; Capital Gains Tax and Class 2 National Insurance do not need to be included (and nor, by the way, do student loan repayments – 'student persecution payments' as my children call them).

There are penalties for fraudulently or negligently reducing payments on account below the level that is genuinely anticipated. However, these penalties will not arise just because you 'get your sums a bit wrong' and slightly underestimate the amount due; they only apply in blatant cases of fraud or negligence. (Estimating rental profits at £10,000 when they actually turn out to be £11,000 is not negligent; forgetting to include any rental income at all, when you know you are receiving it, is!)

When it comes to reduced levels of trading profit, or trading losses being carried back from a later year, it will often be necessary to estimate these on a reasonable basis.

While these estimates need to be reasonable, it is fair for you to take a 'pessimistic' approach to your trading results for the purposes of payments on account.

Being 'reasonably pessimistic' for the purposes of calculating your payments on account, could include:

- Assuming any cash not yet received from trade debtors is a bad debt and will not be received
- Assuming (for accounting purposes) that any payments to your creditors which you are disputing will have to be paid in full
- Assuming (for accounting purposes) that you will have to settle (in full) any customer or employee claims against you that you are disputing
- Writing off the value of trading stock which is perishable (e.g. food), obsolete, old, damaged, etc
- Accruing costs relating to the accounting period for which you have not yet been billed: e.g. utility bills, accountancy fees
- Making a general provision for additional costs relating to the period which you may not yet be aware of

Some of these measures are discussed further in Chapters 15 to 20. Note, however, that general provisions in the final accounts for the period cannot be allowed for tax purposes (but they remain a legitimate part of preparing estimates for the purposes of reducing payments on account).

Example 5.1

Frankie prepares accounts to 31ˢᵗ December each year. To calculate his payments on account for 2020/21, due in January and July 2021, he needs to estimate his profits for the year ended 31ˢᵗ December 2020.

He knows he made sales of £250,000 up to March but, after that, things got rather difficult. His sales for the rest of the year totalled £300,000 and he usually makes a gross profit of 20%, but he suspects it was nearer 15% in this period.

Last year's overheads totalled £25,000 and, as far as he is aware, there is no reason for these to vary significantly.

Lastly, he has a wage bill of £40,000 for the year but this excludes the sum of £10,000 that a former employee is claiming from him.

For the purpose of calculating his payment on account, Frankie estimates his profit for the year as follows:

Gross profit January to March	
£250,000 x 20% =	£50,000
Gross profit April to December	
£300,000 x 15% =	£45,000

Estimated gross profit for year	£95,000
Less:	
Overheads (modest increase assumed)	£26,000
Wages	£40,000
Employee claim	£10,000
General provision for the unknown	£5,000

Estimated taxable profit for year	£14,000

A profit of £14,000 will leave Frankie with an Income Tax liability for 2020/21 of just £300, plus Class 4 National Insurance of £405. These total £705, meaning he can apply to reduce his payment on account due in January 2021 to, say, £350 (£705/2 = £352.50, and it is reasonable to round it down a little).

What Happens if the Estimate is Too Low?

Estimates, by their very nature, will not be precisely accurate. If you have made a reasonable estimate of the tax due, but it later turns out to be too low, you will have to make a balancing payment together with a small amount of interest.

Example 5.2

Frankie makes payments on account of £350 in January and July 2021 in respect of his 2020/21 liability. His actual taxable profits for the year (based on his final accounts for the year ending 31st December 2020) are £16,500. In January 2022, he will have to make the following payments:

Income tax	£800
Class 4 National Insurance	£630
Class 2 National Insurance	£159

	£1,589
Less:	
Payments on account	(£700)

Balancing payment for 2020/21	£889

First payment on account for 2021/22
(£800+£630 = £1,430/2 = £715)   *£715*

Total tax due 31st January 2022   *£1,604*

In addition, his payments on account due for 2020/21 will be automatically adjusted to the correct level of £715 (assuming this is less than the original default position), meaning he underpaid each instalment by £365 (£715 – £350). He will therefore be charged interest as follows:

First instalment for 2020/21
£365 x 3.25%   *£11.86 (12 months late)*
Second instalment for 2020/21
£365 x 3.25% x 6/12   *£5.93   (six months late)*

As we can see, the penalty for slightly underestimating your payments on account is not severe: but I must stress this is in the case of slight underestimates, not negligent underpayments, as discussed above.

It is interesting to note that, when profits rise again (as we would all hope will be the case in 2021), there is no need to increase your payments on account and the 'default position' can be allowed to prevail.

If you overestimate your payments on account, this will lead to a repayment when you submit your tax return for the year or, in most cases, the overpayment will simply be set against your next payment on account.

Example 5.3
Let's stick with the same facts as in Example 5.1 and 5.2 above, but let's now say Frankie didn't include a general provision in his estimated calculations and made payments on account of £1,075 in January and July 2021. His payment in January 2022 will now be as follows:

Final liability for 2020/21   *£1,589*   *(Example 5.2)*
Less:
Payments on account   *(£2,150)*

Balancing repayment due for 2020/21   *(£561)*
First payment on account for 2021/22   *£715*   *(Example 5.2)*

Total net tax due 31st January 2022   *£154*

Frankie would then be deemed to have overpaid his payments on account by £360 (£1,075 - £715) each and would be credited with a small amount of repayment interest (but so small, it's not worth bothering to calculate it!)

Interest on 2020 Payments on Account

As the Government has cancelled the July 2020 payments on account, these sums are now deemed to be due on 31st January 2021, meaning there will be no interest charge provided the relevant amounts are paid by that date.

Taxpayers will be credited with a small amount of repayment interest on any sums paid in January 2020 that turn out to be excessive.

Example 3.2
As we saw previously (Example 3.1 above), Debbie made a payment on account of £10,000 in January 2020. In the end, she did not get around to applying to reduce her 2019/20 payments on account and her final liability for the year (excluding Class 2 National Insurance) turned out to be £11,200. Her first payment on account due on 31st January 2020 is automatically adjusted down to £5,600 (£11,200/2) meaning she overpaid by £4,400. Repayment interest will run on this overpaid sum from 31st January 2020 (the date it was originally due under the 'default position') to 31st January 2021 (the date Debbie's balancing payment for 2019/20 is due).

A Final Word

Reducing your payments on account in line with your expected profits for the relevant period is a sensible thing to do, and by all means include some realistic provisions, accruals, etc, to cover potential additional losses, liabilities, claims, etc. But, overall, we must emphasise: **BE REASONABLE!**

Chapter 12

Changing Your Accounting Date to Save Tax

The ability to change your accounting date may give rise to opportunities for unincorporated businesses to effectively obtain tax relief for losses arising over the next few months more than once. Even periods of reduced profit give rise to significant planning opportunities with the ability to effectively 'bank' lower profit levels at little or no tax cost and cash them in later when your tax rates are higher once more.

These opportunities arise because of the way the Income Tax rules work when an unincorporated business changes its accounting date.

Most trading businesses are free to change their accounting date at least once every six years. This means they will either be shortening an accounting period, or extending it. The maximum permitted length for an accounting period is generally eighteen months. While most businesses use either 5th April or a calendar month end for their accounting date, any date is permissible for a trading business and we will see an example of why a different date (not a calendar month end) may be beneficial later in this chapter.

Sole Traders

It's easier for sole traders to change their accounting date than it is for companies because they don't need to notify Companies House. The consequences of the change can be much more complex, however – although extremely beneficial in some cases.

The sole trader simply draws up accounts to their new accounting date and puts this date on their tax return. For the new date to be effective for tax purposes:

- The tax return must be submitted on time,
- The new accounting period must not exceed eighteen months, and

- Unless the change is made for commercial (non-tax) reasons, there must not have been another earlier change in the previous five tax years

Note that different rules apply for the first three tax years of trading. We looked at these in Chapter 10 and will return to some of the planning opportunities arising later in this chapter.

Short Accounting Period

If you've shortened your accounting period, you will have either one or two accounting dates falling in the tax year. If just one accounting date falls in the tax year, you will be taxed on your profits for the period of twelve months ending on your new accounting date.

This means part of your profits for the previous accounting period will be taxed twice. Any profit that is taxed twice is known as an 'overlap profit'. As we saw in Chapter 10, this also frequently occurs when you start a new business.

Relief for your 'overlap profit' is given when you cease trading, or sometimes on a subsequent change of accounting date. We'll come on to that in a minute.

It may seem like a bad idea to be taxed on the same profit twice, but sometimes you can generate future overlap relief, which could later save you tax at 42% or even more, without paying any, or much, extra tax now.

Example
Gill draws up accounts to 31st March. Her profits for the year ended 31st March 2020 were £40,000. Her profits for the rest of 2020 fell to just £2,500.

Gill decides to shorten her accounting period and prepares accounts for the nine months ended 31st December 2020.Because just one accounting date (31st December 2020) will fall into the 2020/21 tax year, Gill will have to pay tax on her profits for the 12 month period to 31st December 2020.

This means her profits for January to March 2020 will be subject to tax twice – once when she submits her accounts to 31st March 2020 with *her 2020 Tax Return and again when she submits her accounts to 31st December 2020 with her 2021 Tax Return.*

However, because her profits to 31st December 2020 are so low, there is no Income Tax to pay for 2020/21. Her taxable profits are:

Three months to 31st March 2020: 3/12 x £40,000	*£10,000*
Nine months to 31st December 2020:	*£2,500*
Total:	*£12,500*

This is covered by her personal allowance for 2020/21, leaving her with no Income Tax to pay, although it does exceed the National Insurance primary threshold of £9,500 by £3,000, giving her a small Class 4 National Insurance liability of £270 (£3,000 x 9%).

Gill has thus created an overlap of £10,000 available for future use with only minimal current tax cost. If she's a higher rate taxpayer when she ceases trading, this could save her £4,200 (£10,000 x 42%).

If two accounting dates fall in the year, you will be taxed on the profits of both periods. This means you are taxed on more than twelve months of profit in one year, but it also means you may be eligible to claim overlap relief: more on that later.

Long Accounting Periods

If you extend your accounting period, you will either have one accounting date falling in the tax year or none. Where no accounting date falls in the current tax year, you will effectively be taxed on the same twelve months' worth of profit both this year and next year, calculated on a time-apportionment basis.

Example
Hazel normally draws up accounts to 31st March. Her draft accounts for the year ended 31st March 2020 show a profit of £50,000. However, due to losses sustained between March and June 2020, she decides to change her accounting date to 30th June. Her accounts for the fifteen months ending 30th June 2020 show a profit of just £18,000. As no accounting date falls into 2019/20, she is taxed on a profit of £14,400 (£18,000 x 12/15).

Hazel is taxed on the same sum in 2020/21, thus creating an 'overlap profit' of £10,800 (2 x £14,400 – £18,000).

In 2019/20, Hazel will pay Income Tax of £380 (£14,400 less her personal allowance of £12,500, leaving £1,900 taxed at 20%) plus Class 4 National Insurance of £519 (£14,400 less the 2019/20 National Insurance threshold of £8,632, leaving £5,768 taxed at 9%).

In 2020/21, she will again pay Income Tax of £380 but her Class 4 National Insurance will reduce to £441 (£14,400 less the 2020/21 primary threshold of £9,500, leaving £4,900 taxed at 9%).

Hence, ignoring Class 2 National Insurance (which is unaffected by Hazel's change of accounting date), Hazel pays a total of just £1,720 in tax over the course of two years.

If she hadn't changed her accounting date, she would probably have paid little or no tax for 2020/21, but her combined Income Tax and Class 4 National Insurance liability for 2019/20 would have been £11,223. Hence, her change of accounting date has saved her at least £9,500, possibly more.

Furthermore, she has the benefit that tax on profits arising between July and March will now always be deferred by a year and she has overlap relief potentially worth £4,536 (£10,800 x 42%), or even more, to claim in the future.

Using Overlap Relief Now

If you extend your accounting period but your new accounting date still falls in the same tax year, you are taxed on the profits of the whole period. As this is more than twelve months, you can claim relief for some or all of any overlap profit that arose in the past.

Most people whose existing accounting date is not 31st March or 5th April will have overlap profits from when they started trading or from when the self-assessment system began in 1997. You can find your overlap profit in Box 70 on the (full) self-employment pages of your tax return. If there's nothing there check with your accountant: many of them neglect to complete this box as it only affects future periods.

The overlap relief available on a change of accounting date is based on the length of the extended accounting period in excess of twelve months as a proportion of the original period of overlap (but the relief cannot exceed the total overlap profit available).

This means extending your accounting period to a date falling later in the same tax year will be beneficial whenever your profits have fallen below their original level at the time the overlap was created, as will currently be the case for many unincorporated business owners.

Example
Ira has overlap profits brought forward of £45,000 due to a previous overlap period of nine months. He therefore has overlap profits of £5,000 per month.

While his successful business had been producing profits of £12,000 per month until February 2020, his profits have fallen to £1,000 per month. Ira therefore decides to draw up accounts for the eighteen months ended 31st October 2020. The profit shown by his accounts for this period are:

May 2019 to February 2020 @ £12,000 per month	*£120,000*
March to October 2020 @ £1,000 per month	*£8,000*
Total:	*£128,000*

His taxable profit for 2020/21 is therefore:

Profits for period ended 31st October 2020	*£128,000*
Less overlap relief for period in excess of 12 months	
6/9 x £45,000	*£30,000*

Taxable profit:	*£98,000*

If Ira had stuck to his usual accounting date, his taxable profit would have been £122,000 (10 x £12,000 + 2 x £1,000). The change of accounting date has significantly reduced his taxable profit, saving him £14,480 in Income Tax and National Insurance, made up as follows:

Income Tax saved by reducing taxable profit:	
£122,000 – £98,000 = £24,000 @ 40% =	*£9,600*
Income Tax saved by preserving personal allowance*:	
£11,000 @ 40% =	*£4,400*
National Insurance saved by reducing taxable profit:	
£24,000 @ 2% =	*£480*
Total saving:	*£14,480*

* - A profit level of £122,000 would have meant Ira lost £11,000 of his personal allowance for 2020/21 – see Chapter 13

In Ira's case, it is pretty clear that this saving is worthwhile. He has 'cashed in' overlap profits of £30,000 to produce savings at a marginal rate of 42% PLUS a further £4,400 derived from preserving his personal allowance. That's an overall rate of saving of 56.7%, which would be hard to beat.

[If you're wondering why I get 56.7% when £14,480/£30,000 actually equates to 48.3% (still pretty good) it's because we also have to remember that an additional £6,000 of profit arising between May and October 2020 is being taxed at 42% in 2020/21 – and would (probably) have been taxed at the same rate in 2021/22 in any case if Ira's business recovered to its usual profit levels from November 2020 onwards]

In other cases, the decision to 'cash in' overlap profits may be more difficult.

Example
Jackie has overlap profits brought forward of £40,000 due to a previous overlap period of six months. Her profits increased each year taking her to £100,000 in the year ended 30th June 2018, followed by a high of £125,000 for the year ended 30th June 2019. However, for the year ended 30th June 2020, her profits have slumped to £50,000. Even taking this into account, and applying to reduce her payments on account for 2020/21 accordingly (see Chapter 11), her tax bill due on 31st January 2021 will be as follows:

Final liability for 2019/20
(based on profits for year ended 30th June 2019)

Income Tax	*£42,500*
Class 4 National Insurance	*£5,223*
Class 2 National Insurance	*£156*

	£47,879
*Less: Payment on account**	*£16,423*

Balancing payment for 2019/20	*£31,456*
First payment on account for 2020/21	
(based on profits for year ended 30th June 2020)	*£5,573*

Total tax due 31st January 2021	*£37,029*

* - Jackie's payments on account for 2019/20, based on her taxable profit for 2018/19, would have been £16,423 each, but she would only

have made one payment (in January 2020) – see Chapter 11 for further details

Trading conditions remained difficult in the second half of 2020 and Jackie only broke even in this period. As a result, extending her accounting period to 31ˢᵗ December 2020 would leave her taxable profit unaltered at £50,000 but would mean she could claim £40,000 in overlap relief, reducing her 2020/21 tax bill to just £45 in Class 4 National Insurance and £159 in Class 2. Accordingly, she could claim to reduce her payment on account in January 2021 to just £22, saving her £5,551 in valuable cash to help her restore her business (plus another £5,551 in July 2021!)

The drawback here is that Jackie has effectively 'cashed in' her overlap relief at an overall effective rate of just 27.75% (£37,500 @ 29% + £2,500 @ 9% is equivalent to £40,000 at 27.75%). This will be disadvantageous in the long run if her marginal tax rate is higher when she eventually ceases trading. On the other hand, that could be many years away and inflation may have severely eroded the value of her overlap profits by then: a bird in the hand is worth two in the bush!

Cashing in overlap for a saving of 29% now instead of 42% in the future may be the best course of action in some cases: cash is king in these difficult times. But Jackie effectively only got 9% relief on the last £2,500 of her overlap profits: just her Class 4 National Insurance. It may therefore make more sense for her to draw up accounts to a slightly earlier date. Let's say her six months of overlap can be more accurately stated as 182 days. That means her overlap relief equates to £219.78 per day. To limit her overlap relief to £37,500, she therefore needs to extend her accounting period by 170 days (£37,500/£219.78 = 170). Hence, as strange as it may sound, her best option may be to draw up accounts for the period ending 17ᵗʰ December 2020.

See Chapter 10 for full details of how overlap profits are created in the early years of a business, and the periods they cover.

Partnerships

Partnerships can generally change their accounting date in much the same way as sole traders. The impact on each partner will differ, however, as each will have their own individual overlap profit and marginal tax rate. The same change of accounting date could be beneficial for one partner, but disastrous for another. The best thing to do will be to work out the position for each partner and come to a solution that is as mutually beneficial as possible. If there is an overall saving for all the partners taken together, it may be possible to compensate any partners who are 'losing out' by increasing their pre-tax profit share and yet still allow everyone to come out better off in the end.

Limited Liability Partnerships that change their accounting date need to advise Companies House using form LL AA01 and are subject to the same deadlines as a company. Generally, the change must be notified by the earliest of:

- Nine months from the new accounting date
- Nine months from the existing accounting date
- 21 months from the date of incorporation

And before accounts have been filed for the old accounting date!

Early Years
As explained in Chapter 10, different rules apply in the first three tax years of a trading business. However, opportunities to save tax may still arise.

Example
Karen started trading in August 2018. At first, she decided to keep life simple, and began drawing up accounts to 31st March each year. Up to mid-March 2020, things were going well and, despite the impact of the Coronavirus Crisis in the second half of that month, her accounts for the year ended 31st March 2020 showed a profit of £80,000.

However, for the period from April to August 2020, Karen made a loss of £12,000. Business then improved with £5,000 per month profit from September to December 2020, rising to £7,500 per month thereafter.

If Karen sticks with her 31st March year end, her results will be as follows:

Year to 31· March 2020, profit £80,000, taxed in 2019/20, total tax £23,979*

Year to 31· March 2021, profit £30,500, taxed in 2020/21, total tax £5,649*

Year to 31· March 2022, profit £90,000, taxed in 2021/22, total tax £28,104*

Like many people, Karen is going to face a massive tax bill on 31st January 2021, due to her still healthy profits for the year ended 31st March 2020.

So, she decides 'to hell with keeping things simple', draws up a set of accounts for the seventeen months ended 31st August 2020 and adopts 31st August as her accounting date thereafter. She now reports the following results:

Period ended 31st August 2020, profit of £68,000
Year ended 31st August 2021, profit of £80,000

Following the principles explained in Chapter 10, this is taxed as follows:

2019/20
Taxable profit is £68,000 x 12/17 = £48,000, total tax £10,799*

2020/21
Taxable profit is again £68,000 x 12/17 = £48,000, total tax £10,724*

2021/22
Taxable profit is £80,000, total tax bill £23,904*

Karen's total tax bill over the three years is reduced from £57,732 to £45,427: a cumulative saving of £12,305.

Perhaps more importantly, her 2019/20 tax bill due on 31st January 2021 will be reduced by £13,180 (£23,979 – £10,799), although her payments on account in January and July 2021 can only be reduced to £5,321 (half of her 2020/21 tax bill, as above, after excluding Class 2 NI). Originally, she could have reduced these to £2,784. Nonetheless, the net cashflow saving in January 2021 remains £10,643.

There are other benefits for Karen too. The tax on her rising profit levels is effectively deferred (tax on future profits arising between September and March every year is deferred by twelve months). In addition, she has created an overlap profit of £28,000 (£48,000 x 2 – £68,000), which may provide tax relief at 42%, or even more, at some time in the future.

* - Income Tax, Class 4 and Class 2 National Insurance; 2021/22 calculated at 2020/21 rates (but see Chapter 2 regarding potential future tax rates)

Chapter 13

Introduction to Marginal Rate Tax Planning

Accountants and tax advisers often talk about 'marginal tax rates' and 'marginal rate planning'. What do these phrases mean, and why do they matter?

Your 'marginal tax rate' is the rate of tax you are paying on the top part of your income. Put another way, it is the extra tax you pay on each additional pound of income. Hence, for example, a marginal tax rate of 42% means you pay another 42p in tax on an additional pound of income.

Perhaps more importantly, your marginal tax rate also measures how much tax you will save by reducing your taxable income by a pound. For example, a marginal tax rate of 62% means you can save 62p by reducing your taxable income by a pound.

Marginal tax rates are particularly important if you are:

- Assessing the value of a tax-saving measure (such as buying equipment to benefit from the Annual Investment Allowance – see Chapter 6)
- Moving taxable income from one person to another (such as when you pay your children a salary – see Chapter 5)
- Deferring taxable income into a later year
- Accelerating taxable income into an earlier year
- Accelerating deductible expenses into an earlier year
- Deferring deductible expenses into a later year

Most of these planning measures involve exchanging one marginal tax rate for another. As long as income or profits end up being taxed at a lower rate, tax will be saved and the planning is effective. For example, if your marginal tax rate for 2020/21 is 29%, but will rise to 42% in 2021/22, deferring deductible expenditure into 2021/22 will provide you with an extra saving of 13%.

This type of planning is likely to be critical over the next year or so, as many people are likely to see their marginal tax rates fall (typically being less in 2020/21 than in 2019/20) and then hopefully rise again (typically, one hopes, being higher in 2021/22 than in 2020/21). For this reason, in this chapter, we will take a thorough look at marginal tax rates and how they work in practice.

Over the next few chapters, we will then look at a variety of measures which put marginal rate planning into effect. First, however, we need to look at what your marginal tax rates are. These depend on a number of factors:

- Which tax year the income is taxable in
- What type of income you have
- What your total income for the tax year is
- Whether you live in Scotland (tax rates are different for Scottish taxpayers and we will look at these in Chapter 27)

In this guide, we are mostly concerned with the marginal tax rates for 2019/20 and 2020/21, and these are set out in the tables below. But what creates these marginal rates?

Firstly, of course, we have the main Income Tax rates. The official rates applying to all income except interest, savings and dividend income, after deduction of the personal allowance, are as follows:

Official Income Tax Rates after Deducting Personal Allowance

2019/20	2020/21	Tax Rate	
First £37,500	First £37,500	20%	Basic rate
£37,500 to £150,000	£37,500 to £150,000	40%	Higher rate
Over £150,000	Over £150,000	45%	Additional rate

However, to apply these rates in practice, we have to first factor in the personal allowance; then factor in its withdrawal on income in excess of £100,000. For each £2 by which total taxable income exceeds £100,000, the taxpayer loses £1 of their personal allowance. This creates a marginal Income Tax rate of 60% on most income falling into the band between £100,000 and £125,000 in both 2019/20 and 2020/21.

Adding these factors produces the more familiar Income Tax bands and allowances set out in the Appendix, including the all-important higher-rate tax threshold of £50,000 in both 2019/20 and 2020/21.

If you want to see the main marginal tax rates for Income Tax alone see the table for 'Rental Profits and Pension Income' below. For those over state pension age (approximately 66 at present), these marginal tax rates also apply to employment income and self-employment trading income.

Another factor critical to many taxpayers is the High Income Child Benefit Charge. Where this charge applies, it creates even higher marginal tax rates on income between £50,000 and £60,000 received by the highest earner in the household. We will look at the application of the charge, and the resultant marginal tax rates, in Chapter 44, but have ignored it for the purposes of the tables set out in this chapter.

In addition to Income Tax, taxpayers under state pension age in receipt of employment income are subject to Class 1 National Insurance at 12% on income between the primary threshold and the upper earnings limit. Class 1 National Insurance at 2% is then payable on income in excess of the upper earnings limit.

Taxpayers under state pension age with self-employment trading profits are subject to Class 4 National Insurance at 9% on profits between the primary threshold and the upper earnings limit; Class 4 National Insurance at 2% on taxable profits in excess of the upper earnings limit; and Class 2 National Insurance at a fixed weekly rate whenever profits exceed the 'small profits threshold'. Again, these additional charges are in addition to the taxpayer's Income Tax liability.

See Appendix for details of the National Insurance rates and thresholds applying for the tax years 2018/19 to 2020/21.

Interest and savings income is not subject to National Insurance but does have an additional Income Tax rate band, the 'starting rate band' of £5,000. Dividend income has its own, different, set of tax rates.

Marginal Tax Rates – Employment Income under State Pension Age

2019/20	2020/21	Marginal Rate
First £8,632	First £9,500	0%
£8,632 to £12,500	£9,500 to £12,500	12%
£12,500 to £50,000	£12,500 to £50,000	32%
£50,000 to £100,000	£50,000 to £100,000	42%
£100,000 to £125,000	£100,000 to £125,000	62%
£125,000 to £150,000	£125,000 to £150,000	42%
Over £150,000	Over £150,000	47%

Marginal Tax Rates
Self-Employment Trading Income under State Pension Age

2019/20	2020/21	Marginal Rate
First £6,365	First £6,475	0%
£6,365 to £8,632		£156 (2)
	£6,475 to £9,500	£159 (3)
£8,632 to £12,500	£9,500 to £12,500	9%
£12,500 to £50,000	£12,500 to £50,000	29%
£50,000 to £100,000	£50,000 to £100,000	42%
£100,000 to £125,000	£100,000 to £125,000	62%
£125,000 to £150,000	£125,000 to £150,000	42%
Over £150,000	Over £150,000	47%

Notes
1. Includes partnership trading income
2. Class 2 National Insurance at £3.00 per week
3. Class 2 National Insurance at £3.05 per week

Marginal Tax Rates – Rental Profits and Pension Income

2019/20	2020/21	Marginal Rate
First £12,500	First £12,500	0%
£12,500 to £50,000	£12,500 to £50,000	20%
£50,000 to £100,000	£50,000 to £100,000	40%
£100,000 to £125,000	£100,000 to £125,000	60%
£125,000 to £150,000	£125,000 to £150,000	40%
Over £150,000	Over £150,000	45%

Notes
1. The same rates apply to employment income or self-employment trading profits received by taxpayers over state pension age
2. Rental 'profits' for residential landlords (excluding furnished holiday lets) are after deducting only 25% of eligible interest and finance costs in 2019/20 and before deducting **any** interest and finance costs in 2020/21. Eligible costs not permitted as a deduction are relieved at basic rate (20%) but this generally has no effect on marginal tax rates. See Chapter 21 for an examination of the impact this has on marginal rate planning for landlords and see the Taxcafe.co.uk guide *How to Save Property Tax* for further details on this complex subject.

Marginal Tax Rates – Interest and Savings Income

2019/20	2020/21	Marginal Rate
First £12,500	First £12,500	0%
£12,500 to £17,500	£12,500 to £17,500	0% (2)
£17,500 to £50,000	£17,500 to £50,000	20%
£50,000 to £100,000	£50,000 to £100,000	40%
£100,000 to £125,000	£100,000 to £125,000	60%
£125,000 to £150,000	£125,000 to £150,000	40%
Over £150,000	Over £150,000	45%

Notes
1. The Personal Savings Allowance exempts basic rate taxpayers from tax on the first £1,000 of interest and savings income which would otherwise be subject to tax at more than 0%. The allowance reduces to £500 for higher-rate taxpayers and is not available at all to additional rate taxpayers
2. The starting rate band applies only when interest and savings income falls within it. This concept is explained further below.

Marginal Tax Rates – Dividend Income

2019/20	2020/21	Marginal Rate
First £12,500	First £12,500	0%
£12,500 to £50,000	£12,500 to £50,000	7.5%
£50,000 to £100,000	£50,000 to £100,000	32.5%
£100,000 to £125,000	£100,000 to £125,000	48.75% to 65% (2)
£125,000 to £150,000	£125,000 to £150,000	32.5%
Over £150,000	Over £150,000	38.1%

Notes
1. The dividend allowance (£2,000 in both 2019/20 and 2020/21) exempts the first £2,000 of dividend income not covered by the personal allowance, whichever tax band it falls into
2. The effective marginal tax rate on dividend income falling into this band depends on what other types of income the taxpayer has

Taxpayers with a Single Source of Income

If you have only one source of income, the marginal tax rate tables set out above are easy to apply. For example, if all you receive is rental income, you can simply follow the 'Rental Profits and Pension Income' table above. Hence a landlord with taxable rental profits of £60,000 has a marginal tax rate of 40%; a landlord with taxable rental profits of £40,000 has a marginal tax rate of 20%, and so on.

Similarly, a self-employed sole trader (or partner in receipt of trading profits) who has no other sources of income can simply follow the 'Self-Employment Trading Income' table above. Hence a self-employed taxpayer with trading profits of £35,000 has a marginal tax rate of 29%; a self-employed taxpayer with trading profits of £105,000 has a marginal tax rate of 62%, and so on.

Taxpayers with Multiple Sources of Income

Where you have more than one source of income things can become a bit more complex, as we need to factor in the order in which different types of income are taxed. This order is as follows:

i)   Earned income (employment/self-employment trading income)
ii)   Rental and pension income
iii)   Interest and savings income
iv)   Dividend income

Generally speaking, this ordering means the marginal tax rate on each source of income is the rate for the top band which that source of income falls into: but there are exceptions!

Example 1
For the tax year 2020/21, Mandy has a salary of £40,000, taxable rental profits of £15,000, interest income of £1,000 and dividend income of £7,500.

Applying our marginal rate tables, we must treat this income as follows:
Her salary is the first £40,000 of her income
Her taxable rental profits represent income from £40,000 to £55,000
Her interest income represents income from £55,000 to £56,000
Her dividend income represents income from £56,000 to £63,500

Applying our tables, this means an extra £1,000 of income would increase Mandy's tax bill by:

£325 (32.5%) if her dividend income were increased
£400 (40%) if her interest income were increased
£400 (40%) if her rental profits were increased

However, the position for her salary income is more complicated. An extra £1,000 of salary would attract Income Tax and National Insurance at a combined rate of 32%, but this extra income would also push a further £1,000 of Mandy's rental profits out of the 20% band and into the 40% band, costing a further £200, or 20%. The overall effective marginal rate on her salary income is therefore 52%.

Nonetheless, our marginal rate tables are still providing the correct marginal rates for most of Mandy's income sources, and it is unlikely she is able to vary her employment income in any case (unless she is a director of her own company, a subject covered in detail in Chapter 3).

Things can get even more complex, especially for taxpayers with both self-employed trading profits and other sources of income.

Example 2
For the tax year 2020/21, Lisa has self-employment trading profits of £25,000, taxable rental profits of £20,000, interest income of £2,000 and dividend income of £9,000.

In applying our marginal rate tables, we treat this income as follows:

Her trading profits are the first £25,000 of her income
Her taxable rental profits represent income from £25,000 to £45,000
Her interest income represents income from £45,000 to £47,000
Her dividend income represents income from £47,000 to £56,000

This produces the following effective tax rates, as per the tables above:

Trading Profits		
First £6,475	0%	£0
£6,475 to £9,500		£159
£9,500 to £12,500	9%	£270
£12,500 to £25,000	29%	£3,625
Rental Profits		
£25,000 to £45,000	20%	£4,000
Interest Income		
£45,000 to £45,500*	0%	£0
£45,500 to £47,000	20%	£300
Dividend Income		
£47,000 to £49,000**	0%	£0
£49,000 to £50,000	7.5%	£75
£50,000 to £56,000	32.5%	£1,950
Total Tax Suffered		**£10,379**

* - *Lisa's personal savings allowance is reduced to £500 because her dividend income has made her a higher-rate taxpayer. She is not entitled to the starting rate band on her interest income because her salary has already used up the income band from £12,500 to £17,500.*
** - *The dividend allowance*

But What is Lisa's Marginal Tax Rate?

Lisa's marginal rate depends on what type of income we are looking at. For the top part of her income, dividends in this case, it is simply her top rate of tax, 32.5%. So, £1,000 less dividend income will reduce her tax bill by 32.5%, or £325. But what happens if we change one of her other sources of income? Let's do that with each type of income in turn and see what effect it has on her tax bill. Let's start by reducing her interest income by £1,000. This changes her tax liabilities as follows:

Trading Profits		
First £6,475	0%	£0
£6,475 to £9,500		£159
£9,500 to £12,500	9%	£270
£12,500 to £25,000	29%	£3,625
Rental Profits		
£25,000 to £45,000	20%	£4,000
Interest Income		
£45,000 to £45,500	0%	£0
£45,500 to £46,000	20%	£100
Dividend Income		
£46,000 to £48,000	0%	£0
£48,000 to £50,000	7.5%	£150
£50,000 to £55,000	32.5%	£1,625
Total Tax Suffered		*£9,929*

Lisa's tax liability has reduced by £450 (£10,379 – £9,929), meaning the marginal rate on her interest income is actually 45%. This is because she has less interest income taxed at 20% and an extra £1,000 of her dividend income is now also taxed at just 7.5% instead of 32.5%: a further saving of 25%, bringing us up to the total of 45. Reducing interest income is probably difficult, unless the relevant funds giving rise to the interest are passed to a spouse, or the interest was paid by Lisa's own company. Let's now look at something she may have more control over and see what happens if she is able to reduce her taxable rental profits by £1,000 instead:

Trading Profits

First £6,475	0%	£0
£6,475 to £9,500		£159
£9,500 to £12,500	9%	£270
£12,500 to £25,000	29%	£3,625

Rental Profits

£25,000 to £44,000	20%	£3,800

Interest Income

£44,000 to £44,500	0%	£0
£44,500 to £46,000	20%	£300

Dividend Income

£46,000 to £48,000	0%	£0
£48,000 to £50,000	7.5%	£150
£50,000 to £55,000	32.5%	£1,625

Total Tax Suffered   **£9,929**

As we can see, this produces the same result as a reduction in Lisa's interest income. Once again, there is a 20% saving on the reduction itself plus a further 25% saving as a result of an additional £1,000 of dividends being taxed at 7.5% instead of 32.5%; hence, overall, the reduction in Lisa's taxable rental profits leads to a saving of 45% which, in practice, is the effective marginal rate on her rental income.

Lastly, let's look at the impact of a £1,000 reduction in Lisa's self-employment trading profits:

Trading Profits

First £6,475	0%	£0
£6,475 to £9,500		£159
£9,500 to £12,500	9%	£270
£12,500 to £24,000	29%	£3,335

Rental Profits

£24,000 to £44,000	20%	£4,000

Interest Income

£44,000 to £44,500	0%	£0
£44,500 to £46,000	20%	£300

Dividend Income

£46,000 to £48,000	0%	£0
£48,000 to £50,000	7.5%	£150
£50,000 to £55,000	32.5%	£1,625

Total Tax Suffered   **£9,839**

In this case, the reduction in Lisa's trading profits has led to an overall tax saving of £540 (£10,379 – £9,839), indicating an effective marginal rate of 54%. This rate arises as a combination of the 29% saved by reducing taxable trading profits plus the usual additional 25% saving derived from having an extra £1,000 of dividends taxed at 7.5% instead of 32.5%.

As we can see, the best part of her income for Lisa to target if she wishes to generate tax savings is her self-employed rental profits.

Marginal Rate Planning Conclusions

Marginal rate planning is a useful way to save tax overall where your marginal tax rate is expected to change from one tax year to the next. This is likely to be **particularly critical over the next year** or so.

Remember there are 'two sides to the coin' where marginal rate planning involves moving taxable income from one tax year to another (either back to an earlier year, or deferring it to a later year). The planning is only effective where income is moved from a higher marginal rate to a lower one.

Marginal rates are relatively simple where you have only one source of income (and can be found in the tables above) but become more complex where you have multiples sources.

Where multiple sources of income exist, your tax changes (reductions or increases) may vary, according to which source of income you change. The greatest tax changes will ***generally*** come by following this order of priority:

i)   Employment income (although many people cannot influence this)
ii)   Self-employment trading profits
iii)   Taxable rental profits, pension income, or interest and savings income
iv)   Dividend income

Naturally, you can only change sources of income that you have some control over, such as:

- Salary, dividends, or interest paid to you by your own company
- Self-employment trading income
- Rental profits
- Pension income that can be deferred or private pension funds that can be 'cashed in' early

Furthermore, it is probable many people are more likely to save tax overall by increasing their taxable income in 2020/21, either by deferring income from 2019/20 into 2020/21, or by accelerating income from 2021/22 into 2020/21.

In this context, 'income' means taxable income after deducting allowable expenditure. Hence, deferring allowable expenditure is equivalent to accelerating income; and accelerating allowable expenditure is equivalent to deferring income. In the next few chapters, we will look at some of the ways this can be done.

For some, 2021/22 may be the year with the lowest marginal rate, especially owners of trading businesses with accounting dates early in the tax year, such as 30th April (see Chapter 10 for an explanation of how accounting dates and tax years relate to each other).

When it comes to considering probable marginal tax rates for 2021/22 or later years, the rates for 2020/21 are likely to be a good guide, although we have considered potential future tax changes in Chapter 2.

Chapter 14

Putting Marginal Rate Planning into Context

Where your marginal tax rate is set to fall, deferring income or profits into the next tax year is a 'win-win' because it creates **both** a saving and a deferral. For many people this will be the case when looking at deferring income from 2019/20 to 2020/21. If it seems too late to do this, check out Chapters 15 to 19, which show how this might still be accomplished. (Trading businesses also have the option to change their accounting date, which may create similar, or even better, results: see Chapter 12)

Where your marginal tax rate is likely to stay the same, deferring income or profits into the next tax year generally remains beneficial as this still defers payment of tax. However, there can be some unforeseen cashflow consequences in later years. We'll look at the benefits and pitfalls of this type of planning in Chapter 23.

Where your marginal tax rate is set to increase, accelerating income or profits from next year into this year will produce absolute, overall, savings, but will have a detrimental impact on your cashflow as your tax bills will be increased in the short-term. We will look at this 'trade off' in more detail in Chapter 24. This is likely to be relevant to many unincorporated business owners looking to save tax overall in the long term by accelerating profits from 2021/22 into 2020/21.

As I have said before, timings may differ for some taxpayers, who may have a high marginal rate in 2020/21, falling to a lower rate in 2021/22.

Quirks to Watch Out For

Generally speaking, if your profit level reduces from one year to the next, your marginal tax rate will either reduce or stay the same.

There are, however, a couple of quirks in the Income Tax system that mean a reduction in profit can lead to a higher marginal tax rate. These are:

i)   Parents with young children whose taxable profit is over £60,000 one year but falls to somewhere in the £50,000 to £60,000 bracket in the next. These parents' marginal rate in the later year is increased due to the High Income Child Benefit Charge: see Chapter 44 for further details.

ii)   Individuals whose taxable income is over £125,000 one year but falls to somewhere in the £100,000 to £125,000 bracket in the next. This typically creates marginal tax rates of 60% or 62%, higher than those suffered by anyone with income over £125,000.

Hence, for example, an unincorporated business owner with taxable profits of £150,000 in 2019/20, but only £110,000 in 2020/21 would still save tax overall by accelerating income from 2020/21 into 2019/20.

Having said that, if profits are likely to exceed £125,000 again in 2021/22 the best course of action will be to defer income from 2020/21 into 2021/22.

Chapter 15

Action You Can Take after the Accounting Date

You might think there is little you can do to change the results of an accounting period that has already ended. Not so!

For one thing, you may be able to make a significant difference by either joining or leaving the cash basis. You will have until 31st January 2021 to make that decision in respect of the 2019/20 tax year, and we will look at that option for landlords in Chapter 29, and for other unincorporated businesses in Chapter 31. In those chapters, we will also explain how the relevant cash basis differs from traditional 'accruals basis' accounting.

If you remain on the traditional 'accruals basis' of accounting, there is also the possibility of making carefully considered accounting adjustments that may result in the timing of business profits altering slightly. While accounts must be prepared on a reasonable, 'true and fair', basis, there is often some leeway in the exact amount of each accounting adjustment. Over the next few chapters, we will look at some of the items you could consider.

Chapter 16

Bad Debt Relief

There's only one good thing about a bad debt: tax relief. But when is a debt 'bad' and how do you get the most out of the available relief?

Write-offs and Provisions

Bad debt relief generally follows accounting treatment. Where a debt is written off, or a specific accounting provision is made against it, tax relief should usually follow. (Special rules apply to debts between connected parties, e.g. a husband and wife.)

A debt is 'written off' if it is simply removed from the books of the business altogether: i.e. you've given up all hope of recovering it. A 'bad debt provision' is slightly different. This is an accounting adjustment you make to reflect the possibility of not getting paid, but the debt itself stays on the books while you continue to pursue it.

"That sounds great," you may be saying, "I'll make a provision against all my debts and get tax relief for the lot!"

This would not work under traditional 'accruals basis' accounting (but, if this idea appeals to you, you may wish to consider the 'cash basis': see Chapters 29 or 31, as appropriate). Under traditional 'accruals basis' accounting, you are only permitted to make a bad debt provision where there is genuine doubt over the recovery of the debt. If your accounts don't follow generally accepted principles, tax relief would be denied.

However, you can still accelerate relief for bad debts when your accounts are being prepared.

Example 1.1
Nikhil is a landlord with a portfolio of residential properties. His marginal tax rate for 2019/20 was 40%, but he expects it to fall to 20% for 2020/21 as a number of his tenants had to move into smaller properties because they were struggling to pay the rent. Nikhil is seriously worried about his tax bill due on 31st January 2021 and needs to do everything he can to reduce it.

At 5th April 2020, Nikhil was owed £5,000 by Orkim, a good tenant for many years who had run into problems of his own. Orkim has promised repeatedly that he will pay when he gets on his feet but Nikhil is still concerned.

In June, Nikhil is preparing his accounts for 2019/20 and Orkim still hasn't paid his arrears. Nikhil therefore makes a bad debt provision of £5,000 and will obtain tax relief for this in 2019/20, thus reducing his tax bill in January 2021 by £2,000 (£5,000 x 40%).

In February 2021, Orkim is able to pay his rent arrears. Nikhil therefore reverses his bad debt provision in his accounts to 5th April 2021, thus increasing his 2020/21 taxable profits by £5,000. This gives rise to an additional £1,000 (£5,000 x 20%) in tax due on 31st January 2022.

Specific versus General

Some businesses make a 'general provision' to reflect the fact there is always some doubt over the recovery of debts (e.g. 5% of all outstanding debts). During the Coronavirus Crisis, this is probably an appropriate step from a pure accounting perspective, but it is usually a bad idea for tax purposes. This is because a general provision is ineligible for tax relief, whereas a properly calculated specific provision does provide relief.

Example 1.2
Nikhil's other tenants owe a combined total of £10,000 in rent arrears at 5th April 2020. Given the amount of uncertainty at present, he decides to make a further provision of 20% against these other debts – i.e. £2,000.

In July, Nikhil passes his draft accounts to his accountant, Priti, who explains that, while Nikhil will get tax relief for the provision against Orkim's debt, he can't claim relief for his £2,000 general provision.

What Priti also does, however, is to review which of Nikhil's other debts at 5th April are also still outstanding. These sums are now at least 90 days overdue and total £4,000. Priti asks Nikhil if these amounts are likely to be recovered. "Possibly," replies Nikhil, "they're all trying to pay, but I'd say it's about fifty-fifty whether they'll manage in the end."

Priti therefore lists the outstanding debts, calculates a provision equal to 50% of the sums outstanding, and includes this in Nikhil's 2019/20 accounts instead of the 20% general provision.

While Priti's provision is the same amount as Nikhil's general provision, it has been properly calculated on a specific basis and is therefore an allowable deduction for tax purposes.

Hence, this leads to a further saving of £800 (£2,000 x 40%) for Nikhil in his January 2021 tax payment, instead of just £400 (£2,000 x 20%) in January 2022.

A little extra effort in accounts preparation pays off in tax relief!

Summing up Nikhil's bad debt provisions, he has now saved a total of £2,800 in tax for 2019/20 and, even if these debts are ultimately paid, it will only cost him an extra £1,400 in his tax bill for 2020/21. Hence, he has both an absolute saving of £1,400 plus an additional cashflow saving of a further £1,400.

Timing of Relief

Where a debt, or any part of it, has almost certainly become irrecoverable, accounting principles require it to be written off or a specific provision to be made in the accounts. In some cases, however, where the recovery is merely doubtful, there may be some flexibility over the timing of tax relief. This will be useful for many taxpayers next year when their marginal tax rates will (hopefully) increase again.

Example 1.3
Nikhil's taxable rental profits for 2020/21 are £40,000 before any bad debt provisions. He expects things to return to normal next year, giving him an expected taxable rental profit of £120,000 for 2021/22. This means his marginal tax rate will increase from 20% in 2020/21 to 60% in 2021/22 (see Chapter 13). Anything he can do to accelerate up to £20,000 extra profit into 2020/21 will provide an ultimate saving of 40%.

At 5th April 2021, many of Nikhil's tenants still owe rent arrears, although all are promising to pay when they get back on their feet. If he makes any bad debt provisions in his accounts to 5th April 2021, he will save tax just 29%. Toshiko would be better off if she just waits to see whether she recovers these debts – any that do go bad during the year to 30th June 2020 will then provide tax relief at 62%.

Do Bad Debt Provisions Really Matter?

Some people take the view that a bad debt is really just the same as a sale that never took place, or rent that was never due. This is not the case: there are several important differences.

Accounting principles require the sale to be recognised and total turnover, including these sales, is an important measure for many purposes, including the VAT registration threshold (where applicable) and Companies House filing requirements.

And, as we have seen, bad debts may sometimes yield tax relief at a higher rate than the tax on the original sale or rent!

VAT on Bad Debts

VAT-registered businesses should only make provisions for the net, VAT-exclusive, part of the debt, as the VAT element is not part of your sales and can always be recovered or, in many cases, never paid. For further details on VAT relief for bad debts, see Chapter 25.

Chapter 17

Trading Stock and Work-in-Progress

The biggest deduction in many trading business's accounts is cost of sales. Unfortunately, that deduction is itself also subject to a deduction: closing stock and work-in-progress.

A deduction from a deduction means an increase in taxable profits and we can save tax by reducing it as much as possible. Alternatively, where your marginal tax rate (see Chapter 13) is set to increase next year, you may wish to increase the value of closing stock and work-in-progress as much as possible this year, thus bringing profits forward to benefit from a lower marginal tax rate.

Closing stock is a measure of the value of goods still on hand or services not yet completed at the accounting date. The treatment of goods and services differs a little. In this chapter, we are going to look at goods: tangible products which the business sells. We will look at services in Chapter 18.

Closing stock needs to be valued at the lower of cost or 'net realisable value'. Let's look at cost first.

Direct Costs Only

The stock figure in your accounts only needs to include the direct costs of acquiring or producing your product, so the first thing to do is to look at your costing system and make sure that you're not including any indirect costs.

You do, however, need to include production overheads, such as factory or workshop electricity costs and business rates. The electricity or business rates for an office would, however, usually be an indirect cost and should generally be excluded.

Many small businesses will not pay business rates in 2020/21, so this may have an impact on stock valuations at your next accounting date.

Net Realisable Value

Let's say it has cost you £100 to make a product and you would normally sell it for £120. However, to sell the product, you will need to incur advertising and other costs of £10. This still leaves you a profit so you would continue to value the stock of this product at £100.

Let's suppose, however, that a competitor launches a better product, so you can only sell yours for £105 and your advertising and other selling costs increase to £25. The product now has a net realisable value of £80 (£105 - £25).

In effect, you know that you are now going to make a loss on this product. You are allowed to anticipate this loss by reducing your stock value in your accounts to just £80. This will effectively give you tax relief of £20 per item now, even before you sell the product.

It is often worth having a good look at your stock to see which items can be valued at less than cost in order to provide tax relief for your effective loss now. Things to look out for include:

- Old or damaged goods which are no longer usable
- Perishable goods which you will be unable to sell
- Obsolete stock superseded by changes in fashion or technology
- Surplus stock for which there is no demand
- Missing items (perhaps lost or stolen)

Example 1.1
Ruben runs a small restaurant. He had to close in mid-March 2020. Nonetheless, his accounts for the year ended 31ˢᵗ March 2020 still show a profit of £75,000, making him a higher-rate taxpayer for 2019/20. Due to the Coronavirus Crisis, he expects to be a basic rate taxpayer for 2020/21.

When Ruben returns to the restaurant in the summer, he has to throw away £10,000 worth of stock which is no longer usable. He deducts this sum from his closing stock at 31ˢᵗ March 2020, thus reducing his taxable profits in 2019/20 to £65,000 and saving him £4,200 in Income Tax and National Insurance at a combined rate of 42%.

If he had put this loss through in his March 2021 accounts, it would only have produced relief at a combined rate of 29%, or £2,900. Hence, not only does Ruben reduce his tax bill on 31st January 2021 by £4,200, he also makes an absolute, permanent saving of £1,300.

It's Only a Matter of Time

Although the savings yielded by reducing stock value can be worthwhile, they are sometimes only temporary. If your marginal tax rate is the same next year as it is this year, you will simply have deferred tax, not saved any. Even so, this may still be worthwhile, as we will see in Chapter 23.

But many business owners, like Ruben in our example, may have a lower tax rate in 2020/21 than in 2019/20, making it highly beneficial to reduce stock values in their accounts for accounting dates falling in 2019/20.

The position is different if you anticipate having a higher tax rate next year than this year, such as when your profits are increasing again after the Coronavirus Crisis. In these cases, a reduction in the value of your stock will give rise to an overall tax cost. You still need to apply the same principles to valuing your stock but you might want to take a more optimistic (but reasonable) view of its net realisable value.

Example 1.2
After struggling through 2020/21, Ruben's business picks up dramatically in the spring of 2021. So much so, he anticipates taxable profits of £110,000 in 2021/22.

When he gives his draft accounts to his accountant, Rebecca, she points out that he has an excessive amount of tinned soup in stock at 31st March 2021 and suggests that 90% of its value be written off as he is unlikely to sell it all. This would mean reducing his profits for 2020/21 by £5,000, which would reduce his tax bill by £1,450 (29%) but it would also increase his profits for 2021/22 by the same amount, costing him an extra £3,100 (at 62% - see Chapter 13).

However, later in 2021, Ruben launches a lunchtime 'soup and roll' special which is very successful. He sells most of his stock of soup and Rebecca accepts there is no need to adjust his accounts at 31st March 2021. Although he has an extra £1,450 to pay in January 2022, he has £3,100 less to pay in January 2023, an overall saving of £1,650.

Chapter 18

Work in Progress for Service Businesses

Businesses, such as accountants, lawyers, surveyors, graphic designers, and others providing services under a contract are required to include a value for their work-in-progress in their accounts. This is the estimated value of the work carried out to date, as a proportion of the eventual sale price. For example, if a graphic designer is half-way through completing a project with a contracted fee of £1,000, they should include working-in-progress of £500 in their accounts.

The tax planning principles around valuing work in progress in a service business are exactly the same as for a trading business holding physical goods, which we examined in Chapter 17: namely, if marginal tax rates are expected to fall or remain the same next year, it is preferable to value work-in-progress as low as is reasonable at the accounting date; or, if marginal tax rates are expected to increase next year, it may be preferable to value work-in-progress as high as possible.

Factors to consider when valuing work-in-progress include:

- Any doubt over the customer's ability, or willingness, to pay
- Costs still to be incurred on the project (remember the 'net realisable value' principle discussed in Chapter 17)
- Administration and other costs relating to completion of the sale and collection of the fee

There is also a strong argument that a half-completed job is not worth anywhere near as much as half the fee for a completed job.

Taking all these factors into account, an appropriate value for our graphic designer's half completed job might be nearer to £300. On the other hand, in some cases, he might prefer to argue that the difficult part of the job is already done and it's just routine from here, so a value of £750 might be more appropriate.

Chapter 19

Accruals, Provisions and Prepayments

We've looked at bad debts, trading stock and work-in-progress. Businesses operating under traditional 'accruals basis' accounting are also required to make reasonable accruals and provisions for costs relating to the accounting period that have not yet been invoiced, billed or paid at the accounting date. These are called accruals or provisions and typically include:

- Employee's wages for days worked before (or on) the accounting date but paid later
- Staff bonuses in respect of the accounting period (these must actually be paid within nine months of the accounting date to be allowed for tax purposes – see further in Chapter 3)
- Employees' accrued holiday pay
- Unclaimed employees' expenses (e.g. business mileage claims)
- Accountancy fees incurred to date and:
  - o Further fees to prepare and finalise the accounts for the period
  - o Fees for any VAT returns or payroll services which are wholly or partly for periods falling within the business's accounting period
  - o Fees for the completion and submission of tax returns for the period (either for Income Tax or Corporation Tax, as the case may be)
- Utility bills covering part of the accounting period
- Legal and professional fees not yet invoiced
- Repairs and maintenance costs not yet invoiced
- Customer returns or credit notes to be issued
- Legal claims against the business
- Banks charges and interest on loans, including hire purchase agreements

To be allowed for tax purposes, a provision must be calculated on a specific basis, using the most reasonable estimates available at the time the accounts are being prepared. General provisions for unexpected additional costs are not allowed for tax purposes (although they could be useful in reducing payments on account, as discussed in Chapter 11).

Generally the costs must effectively have arisen at the accounting date. However, a provision for future repairs or maintenance costs can be allowed if:

i)   There is a legal or contractual obligation to incur the expenditure,

ii)   There is a specific programme of repair work to be undertaken, and

iii)   The accounting provision has been computed with a reasonable degree of accuracy

The cost of getting a van through its MOT might sometimes meet these requirements, for example.

As with all year-end accounting adjustments, there is often a degree of estimation involved in computing accruals and provisions and there is some leeway in the exact amounts to be included in the final accounts. Hence, one might like to 'err on the side of caution' when marginal tax rates are about to fall next year, or even when they are likely to stay the same; but take a more optimistic view when next year's marginal rate looks set to be higher.

The Employment Allowance

One that is often forgotten is the employment allowance. In 2020/21, the allowance will cover the first £4,000 of employer's National Insurance payable in the tax year. The allowance always operates according to the tax year, regardless of what the employer's own accounting period is. Hence, for businesses that do not have a 31st March or 5th April accounting period, the allowance does not properly match the results for the period: unless an accounting adjustment is made to reflect this.

Example
Susan runs a general store, selling food and other essentials. She stays open during the Coronavirus Crisis and will make a healthy profit for the year ended 30th June 2020, making her a higher-rate taxpayer for 2020/21. In the period from 6th April to 30th June, she would have paid £3,200 in employer's National Insurance if it had not been for the

employment allowance. However, thanks to the allowance, she did not pay any employer's National Insurance for this period.

However, under traditional 'accruals basis' accounting we should allocate the employment allowance over the whole of the 2020/21 tax year. This means only £1,000 (3/12 x £4,000) should be allocated to the period from April to June. Susan can therefore quite rightly accrue a cost of £2,200 (£3,200 – £1,000) in her accounts to 30th June 2020, representing the true employer's National Insurance cost for this period. This correct adjustment saves Susan £924 in Income Tax and National Insurance (at 42%).

Prepayments

Prepayments are the opposite of accruals: costs you've already paid but which wholly or partly relate to a later accounting period. By classing part of the amount already paid as a prepayment, you will defer part of the expense to the next accounting period, thus increasing this year's taxable profits and reducing next year's.

This is correct accounting procedure at any time but, if you are expecting to have a higher marginal tax rate next year, you might just want to try that little bit harder to identify as many prepayments as possible.

Typical items to consider include:

- Insurance premiums
- Subscriptions
- Vehicle excise duty (road tax)
- Standing charges within utility bills
- Rent paid (especially if quarterly)
- Finance charges on long-term loans

Chapter 20

Year End Planning (Action before the Accounting Date)

In this chapter we will take a look at a variety of year-end tax planning strategies that generally need to be implemented before your accounting date. Hence, it will generally be too late to implement these strategies for accounting periods falling to be taxed in 2019/20 (except where some of the rules explored in Chapters 10 and 12 apply to the 'early years' of a trading business or changes of accounting date).

The strategies in this chapter will, however, be useful for many people wishing to either increase or decrease their taxable profits for 2020/21 (see Chapters 13, 14 and 24 for an explanation of why you might want to increase your taxable profits and the consequences that need to be weighed up).

We will start, however, with the more common aim (in normal times) of reducing taxable profits.

Reducing this Year's Taxable Profits

By deferring income for just one day, it may be possible to postpone tax for a whole year; by accelerating expenses, it is often possible to enjoy tax relief one year earlier. Year-end tax planning is even more powerful if you expect your tax rate to fall for the next year: you will not only be postponing tax, you will be saving it as well.

Business Year-End Planning

In this chapter, we are going to focus on business year-end planning: where your own accounting date is the key date. This type of planning is equally relevant to companies, partnerships, sole traders and landlords.

For example, a sole trader or partnership with a 30th June accounting date needs to take action by 30th June 2020 to save tax for 2020/21; a company with a 31st December accounting date needs to take action by 31st December 2020 to reduce its Corporation Tax bill due on 1st October 2021; and an individual landlord will generally have until 5th April 2021 to implement measures to save tax for 2020/21.

Business year-end tax planning should generally only be about accelerating the expenditure you need to make anyway: it's seldom worth spending extra money just to save tax.

Accelerating Expenses

Any liabilities incurred by your accounting date can reduce your taxable profits, even if you only pay the bill later. In a few instances, where there is a legal obligation to have work carried out, just getting a quote by your accounting date may be enough – repairs required to get an M.O.T. certificate on a van would be a good example.

An easy way to reduce your tax bill is to buy large items that enjoy an immediate 100% deduction under the annual investment allowance. Examples include vans, computers and office equipment. Integral features in commercial property also qualify, including wiring, lighting, plumbing, heating and air-conditioning. This idea is explored further in Chapter 6.

Cars

Cars are another item that can help business owners cut their tax bills. You can currently claim up to 18% of the cost as a tax deduction in the accounting period you purchase the car (6% if the car has CO_2 emissions over 110g/km).

For self-employed business owners, the allowance is restricted to reflect private use, but even just one quarter business use of a £25,000 car could give you a deduction of £1,125.

New cars with CO_2 emissions of 50g/km or less are currently eligible for an immediate 100% enhanced capital allowance: the potential tax saving benefits of this are explored further in Chapter 6.

If you are selling a car, you will also often benefit by completing the transaction before your accounting date. Sales of cars often give rise to balancing allowances which can sometimes significantly reduce your taxable profits. (Beware, however, that balancing charges can also sometimes arise: so do your sums first.)

Business Property (including Rental Property)

If you own business premises or rental property, one of the best ways to save tax is to carry out repairs before your accounting date.

Anything classed as an improvement is less help, as tax relief on this expenditure may only be given at 3% per year on commercial property, thanks to the new structures and buildings allowance, and no relief at all is available on residential property.

Anything qualifying as an 'integral feature' may attract 100% tax relief under the annual investment allowance: see Chapter 6.

Some types of property expenditure are often classed as repairs for tax purposes BUT may still increase the value of your property: such as replacement kitchens or bathrooms, double glazing, re-wiring and decorating. Many property owners think of these items as improvements, but they are often fully tax deductible repairs, providing you follow the rules. (See the Taxcafe.co.uk guide *How to Save Property Tax* for more information.)

Other Business Expenditure

Simply purchasing more trading stock before your accounting date will not generally alter your taxable profits (unless you are using cash accounting – see Chapter 31).

Utility bills, interest costs, and many other items are all effectively time-related, so it is not generally possible to accelerate these. It remains important to include accruals in respect of these costs, where appropriate, however (see Chapter 19). Again, the position is different if you are using cash accounting.

Nonetheless, there are some items of expenditure that can sometimes be accelerated in order to provide earlier tax relief. Naturally, this is only worth considering where funds are available and there are little or no adverse commercial implications to making the expenditure earlier. Subject to these points, items worth considering include:

- Repairs and maintenance (we covered business property above, but think about machinery, equipment, and vehicles as well: if funds permit, this might be a good time to take equipment 'off line' and carry out additional maintenance)
- Top business vehicles and company cars up with fuel
- Make business journeys (such as visiting customers – naturally we are talking about *after* the immediate Coronavirus Crisis has passed)
- Staff entertaining (again, *after* the immediate Coronavirus Crisis)
- Advertising and promotion
- Employee bonuses (where these are discretionary or gratuitous, rather than contractual)
- Staff recruitment (agents' commission will generally be a deductible expense)
- Legal and professional costs, such as business advice, or consultancy (provided these are not capital expenditure, or personal expenditure to benefit the business owner, and could not otherwise have been accrued at the accounting date in any case – such as accountant's fees for preparing your annual accounts)

Some of these items may be difficult to do at the moment (and some are absolutely out of the question) but these items may be relevant for later accounting dates, such as 31st December 2020 or 31st March 2021.

But remember, as always, it is generally only worth accelerating expenditure that you are going to make anyway.

Deferring Income

For businesses supplying goods, it makes sense to consider delaying the completion of sales until after the accounting date, so the profit falls into the next period. Commercial pressures will often dictate the opposite, however!

Sadly, for businesses supplying services, deferring income is not so easy and this point is covered in Chapter 18. However, where commercial pressures allow, you could still consider putting off some work until after your year end, so that the income 'earned' by that date is less. Most people would agree that two half-finished jobs are worth less than one completed one.

Increasing this Year's Taxable Profits

If you expect to be paying tax at a higher rate in the next tax year, it may be better to do the complete opposite: accelerate your income and defer your expenses. The marginal rate tables in Chapter 13 will help you see whether this action might be appropriate for you and, in Chapter 24 we will look at some of the practical consequences.

Those who may wish to consider reversing their year-end tax planning in this way include unincorporated trading business owners expecting their marginal tax rate to rise from 29% to 42%; from 42% to 47%; or from 42% to 62%; and landlords expecting their marginal tax rate to rise from 20% to 40%; from 40% to 45%; or from 40% to 60%.

How to Accelerate Income and Defer Expenses

If you expect your marginal tax rate to rise next year, you may wish to consider accelerating income or deferring expenses in order to bring more taxable income into the current year and thus save tax overall. Some of the techniques you could consider include:

- Defer capital expenditure in order to claim the annual investment allowance next year instead of this year (but see Chapter 6 regarding the transitional rules that may potentially apply in the early months of 2021)
- Defer other non-essential/non-urgent business expenditure, including discretionary repairs and maintenance expenditure and other non-urgent items, as listed above under 'Other Business Expenditure'
- Defer gift aid and pension contributions to after 5th April
- Complete orders and projects and bring billing up to date. Accounting rules often require part-completed work to be brought into account, but there is still a large element of profit dependent on completion and billing in many cases. For example, two half completed projects are, in accounting terms, likely to yield less profit than a single completed project of the same size
- Connected businesses (e.g. wife has business, husband also has his own business): make extra sales to connected businesses in advance of year end

- Defer *the sale* of a car that will give rise to a balancing allowance (but accelerate the sale of car that will give rise to a balancing charge)

Should Car Purchases be Deferred to Accelerate Taxable Profit?

Deferring *the purchase* of most cars will not really help to accelerate profit from next year into this, except in the case of all electric cars with zero CO2 emissions (see Chapter 6). For cars with CO2 emissions above zero, but not exceeding 110g/km, a delay in purchasing the car until after 31st March 2021 would be extremely counter-productive, as the rate of capital allowances available will fall thereafter (the rate on cars with CO2 emissions above zero but not exceeding 50g/km will fall from 100% to 18%; the rate on cars with CO2 emissions exceeding 50g/km but not exceeding 110g/km will fall from 18% to 6%).

In other cases, deferring the purchase will have a less significant effect but will generally still not be beneficial. At least not in the short-term anyway.

Example

Tracy is a sole trader and expects her accounts for the year ending 31st December 2020 to show a profit of just £30,000, making her a basic rate taxpayer with a marginal rate of just 29% for 2020/21. She is a divorced mother with three small children and one consolation is that she will at least be able to claim Child Benefit in 2020/21 without suffering the High Income Child Benefit Charge (see Chapter 44). She is hopeful that her profits for the year ending 31st December 2021 will return to their usual level of around £55,000, but knows that means she will suffer the High Income Child Benefit Charge and will have a marginal tax rate of 67.5% (see Chapter 44).

Tracy is thinking of buying a new car for £20,000. The car will have 75% business use and, as long as she buys it before 1st April 2021, will attract writing down allowances at 18%. However, she wonders if she should delay the purchase until after 31st December to obtain more tax relief.

If she buys the car by 31st December 2020 (and also brings it into use in her business by that date), she will have the following capital allowances, yielding tax savings as follows:

Year ending 31ˢᵗ December 2020:
£20,000 x 18% = £3,600 x 75% = £2,700 writing down allowance
Tax saved @ 29% = £783

Year ending 31ˢᵗ December 2021:
£20,000-£3,600 = £16,400 x 18% = £2,952 x 75% = £2,214 writing down allowance
Tax saved @ 67.5% = £1,494

Hence, the total tax saved over two years is £2,277.

If Tracy waited until after 31ˢᵗ December 2020 to buy the car, she would only get a slightly higher writing down allowance of £2,700 in the year ending 31ˢᵗ December 2021 (instead of £2,214), generating a tax saving of £1,822 (@ 67.5%), which leaves her cumulatively worse off by £455 after two years.

Eventually, of course, the fact that Tracy claimed an extra year's writing down allowance in 2020 will result in a lower balancing allowance (or higher balancing charge) on the sale of the car. If that is likely to be many years away, it may not be worth worrying about. If she changes cars every two or three years, however, this needs to be factored into her decision-making now.

What Doesn't Help to Accelerate Taxable Profit?

Another thing that won't really help accelerate taxable profit is deferring improvement expenditure on commercial property. This expenditure now attracts the Structures and Buildings Allowance at 3%, but deferring it won't help reduce next year's tax bill; it will only reduce the tax bill of whoever owns the property in thirty-three years' time.

Other things may not help to accelerate taxable profit but can at least be deferred to save cash now without affecting taxable profit. We'll look at these in Chapter 22.

Chapter 21

Marginal Rate Planning for Landlords

Most of the principles explored in Chapters 15 to 20 apply equally to landlords, except for issues relating to trading stock and work-in-progress (Chapters 17 and 18). However, residential landlords face an additional factor that complicates matters further.

Since 2017, residential landlords have been losing the ability to deduct mortgage interest and other finance costs from their rental income for tax purposes. Instead, basic rate relief is given for the amounts disallowed. This is leading to significant increases in many landlords' tax bills.

For 2019/20, residential landlords may deduct just 25% of their interest and finance costs, with basic rate relief for the other 75%.

For 2020/21 and later years, residential landlords may only claim basic rate relief for all their interest and finance costs.

Hence, while the Coronavirus Crisis means that many business's taxable profits are reducing, some residential landlords may see their taxable (but not actual) profits increase from 2019/20 to 2020/21. Obviously, this may alter their position as far as marginal rate planning is concerned.

Example
Unnabh is a residential landlord. His accounts show the following:

	2019/20	*2020/21*
Total rental income	*£60,000*	*£55,000*
Less:		
Interest and finance costs	*£32,000*	*£32,000*
Sundry expenditure	*£4,000*	*£1,000*
	----------	----------
True rental profit	*£24,000*	*£22,000*

However, his taxable 'profit' is as follows:

	2019/20	*2020/21*
Total rental income	£60,000	£55,000
Less:		
Interest costs (25%/Nil)	£8,000	-
Sundry expenditure	£4,000	£1,000
Taxable rental profit	£48,000	£54,000

Hence, despite, the fact that his true profits have fallen, Unnabh becomes a higher-rate taxpayer in 2020/21 and his marginal tax rate increases from 20% to 40%. It would therefore make sense for Unnabh to undertake marginal rate planning along the lines discussed in Chapters 13 to 16 and 19.

Note that Unnabh also gets tax relief at 20% for 75% of his interest costs in 2019/20 and all of them in 2020/21. However, this does not alter his marginal tax rate (except in respect of interest and finance costs themselves).

The interest relief restrictions discussed above do not apply to companies, or to furnished holiday letting businesses.

For further details of these dreadful restrictions, see the Taxcafe.co.uk guide *How to Save Property Tax*.

Interest Rate Reductions

Recent reductions in interest rates mean that many landlords may be making higher 'true' rental profits. However, apart from a minor effect in the last few weeks of 2019/20 (when 25% of those costs is still tax deductible as normal), this will not affect individual residential landlords' marginal tax rates due to the fact that, from 2020/21 onwards, these costs can only be relieved at basic rate.

The interest rate reductions may mean higher taxable rental profits for landlords renting out commercial property or landlords operating through a company.

Sadly, owners of furnished holiday lets, while benefitting from the interest rate reductions, are likely to see dramatic falls in their rental profits this year so, for them, marginal rate planning is likely to be similar to many unincorporated trading businesses.

Chapter 22

Saving Cash without Increasing Tax

Many people are short on cash at the moment. What expenditure can you safely defer without causing an increase in your tax bill?

Items worth considering (subject to commercial requirements) include:

1.*   Keep trading stock purchases down to a minimum (as far as possible try to just fill your immediate needs, rather than carrying excess stock) - under traditional 'accruals basis' accounting you will need to include this value in your accounts anyway

2.   Business entertaining (when it is possible again) – this is not allowable anyway

3.   Improvements to residential property – these only attract relief for Capital Gains Tax purposes on an eventual sale

4.   Land purchases

5.   Professional fees that will be treated as capital expenditure, such as architects' fees for a building project, or to obtain planning permission (although these may be a necessary pre-requisite to other expenditure that will produce some form of tax relief)

6.*   Expenditure that can already be accrued anyway (see Chapter 19). If you get your accountant to prepare your accounts for the year ending 30th April 2020 during 2021 instead of later this year (2020), it will not alter the timing of your tax relief for these costs (although these accounts could be useful for applying to reduce your payments on account – see Chapter 11).

* - Deferring this expenditure will increase your tax bill if you are on one of the cash bases (see Chapters 29 and 31)

Many people may be tempted to delay payments to creditors but this could put a strain on business relationships, or even put your suppliers out of business. However, if a delayed payment schedule can be agreed without damaging future business relationships then, if you are on traditional 'accruals basis' accounting, this will not affect your tax liabilities.

Lastly, you may be tempted to delay tax payments. In this context, we would make the following points:

- Some delays have already been sanctioned by the Government, including cancellation of the July 2020 payments on account under self-assessment (see Chapter 11) and deferral of VAT payments due between 20th March and 30th June 2020
- Interest is applied to late payments (currently at 3.25%)
- Delay may also lead to surcharges being applied
- Delays in paying your tax may lead to an increased risk of a tax enquiry
- In cases of genuine hardship, taxpayers can agree delayed payment terms under HMRC's 'time to pay' arrangements (see Chapter 1)

And, furthermore, as we pointed out in the Introduction, the Government needs your tax to provide vital public services and to help get the country back on its feet. So, while we believe you should never pay more than your fair share, we still believe you should pay.

Chapter 23

Deferring Tax Liabilities

In Chapters 15 to 20 we looked at various strategies designed to defer taxable profits into a later year. Where your marginal tax rate in that later year is lower than in the year when the profits would have otherwise been taxed, this produces an absolute overall tax saving.

However, in many cases, your marginal tax rate will remain the same, so we are only looking at a cashflow saving. For companies, this will always be the case, since the Corporation Tax rate has been 19% since April 2017 and will remain so until at least 31st March 2022. Nonetheless, deferring taxable profits into the next accounting period will still delay most companies' Corporation Tax liabilities by a year, so it remains a worthwhile form of tax planning.

What about unincorporated business owners? For them, the payments on account system under self-assessment makes things a little more complex (see Chapter 11 for details). Let's take a look at an example to see how their cashflow savings works in practice.

Example 1
Vicky is a partner in a law firm. The firm draws up accounts to 31st March each year. Her profit share is expected to be as follows:

Year ended 31st March 2019	*£80,000 (Actual)*
Year ended 31st March 2020	*£90,000 (Per draft accounts)*
Year ended 31st March 2021	*£55,000 (Forecast)*
Year ended 31st March 2022	*£75,000 (Forecast)*

Although her profit share falls significantly in 2020/21, she remains a higher-rate taxpayer with the same marginal tax rate each year. Nonetheless, her firm makes some accounting adjustments (see Chapters 15 to 19 for a few tips) that mean £10,000 of her profit share for the year ended 31st March 2020 will now fall in the year ended 31st March 2021 instead. What does this do to her tax payments?

	Before Adjustments	**After Adjustments**
31st January 2021		
Final liability for 2019/20		
Income Tax	£23,500	£19,500
Class 4 National Insurance	£4,523	£4,323
Class 2 National Insurance	£156	£156
	----------	----------
	£28,179	£23,979
Less:		
First payment on account in Jan 2020		
(based on 2018/19 tax bill)	£12,223	£12,223****
	----------	----------
Balancing payment for 2019/20	£15,956	£11,756
First payment on account for 2020/21*	£6,622	£8,722
	----------	----------
Total tax due	£22,578	£20,478
31st July 2021		
Second payment on account		
for 2020/21*	£6,622	£8,722
31st January 2022		
Final liability for 2020/21**		
Income Tax	£9,500	£13,500
Class 4 National Insurance	£4,523	£3,945
Class 2 National Insurance	£159	£159
	----------	----------
	£13,404	£17,604
Less:		
Payments on account	£13,244	£17,444
	----------	----------
Balancing payment for 2020/21	£160	£160
First payment on account		
for 2021/22***	£6,622	£8,722
	----------	----------
Total tax due	£6,782	£8,882
31st July 2022		
Second payment on account for 2021/22***	£6,622	£8,722
Total tax due over two years:	£42,604	£46,804

* Assuming the appropriate claim to reduce payments on account is made (see Chapter 11)
** Assuming original forecast proves correct (subject to adjustments made in 2020 accounts)
*** No reduction is possible as higher profits are anticipated in 2021/22
**** Assuming no claim to reduce this and obtain a repayment was ever made: as seems likely since the repayment would only have amounted to £311, even if it could be substantiated in time (see Chapter 11)

As we can see, the accounting adjustments made in 2020 have yielded a cashflow saving of £2,100 in January 2021. This, in itself may make this course of action worthwhile.

However, because the accounting adjustments result in higher taxable profits for Vicky in 2020/21, and because she is claiming to reduce her payments on account for 2020/21 due to the fact that her profit share is falling, the cashflow saving she enjoys in January 2021 is diminished and, in fact, reverses in July of that year.

Furthermore, because her 2021/22 payments on account are based on her results for 2020/21 (and cannot be reduced), she actually ends up paying an **extra** £4,200 over two years!

Vicky's negative cashflow in 2022 will reverse in January 2023, by which point she will have paid the same amount of tax, in total, as she always would have (because her marginal rate has never changed). Nonetheless, the example shows that year end planning where profits are declining but there is no change in the taxpayer's marginal tax rate, may not be as beneficial as you might imagine.

Even so, that £2,100 saving in January 2021 might be more crucial to Vicky than those higher tax bills in 2022!

The situation is different if profits are on the rise, although the payments on account system will still get its revenge!

Example 2.1
Wendy is another partner in the same firm. She's a bit of a 'rising star', even despite the Coronavirus Crisis, and her profit share was initially expected to be as follows:

Year ended 31st March 2019	*£50,000 (Actual)*
Year ended 31st March 2020	*£65,000 (Per draft accounts)*
Year ended 31st March 2021	*£80,000 (Forecast)*
Year ended 31st March 2022	*£95,000 (Forecast)*

*However, the same accounting adjustments that affected her colleague Vicky will also mean £10,000 of Wendy's profit share for the year ended 31st March 2020 will now fall in the year ended 31st March 2021 instead. What does this do to **her** tax payments?*

	Before Adjustments	**After Adjustments**
31st January 2021		
Final liability for 2019/20		
Income Tax	£13,500	£9,500
Class 4 National Insurance	£4,023	£3,823
Class 2 National Insurance	£156	£156
	---------	---------
	£17,679	£13,479
Less:		
First payment on account made in		
January 2020 (based on 2018/19 tax bill)	£5,923	£5,923
	---------	---------
Balancing payment for 2019/20	£11,756	£7,556
First payment on account for 2020/21	£8,762	£6,662
	---------	---------
Total tax due	£20,518	£14,218
31st July 2021		
Second payment on account for 2020/21	£8,762	£6,662
31st January 2022		
Final liability for 2020/21*		
Income Tax	£19,500	£23,500
Class 4 National Insurance	£4,245	£4,445
Class 2 National Insurance	£159	£159
	---------	---------
	£23,904	£28,104
Less:		
Payments on account	£17,524	£13,324
	---------	---------
Balancing payment for 2020/21	£6,380	£14,780
First payment on account for 2021/22	£11,872	£13,972
	---------	---------
Total tax due	£18,252	£28,752
31st July 2022		
Second payment on account for 2021/22	£11,872	£13,972
Total tax due over two years:	£59,404	£63,604

* Assuming the original forecast proves correct (subject to the adjustments made in the 2020 accounts)

As we can see, Wendy enjoys a massive cashflow advantage in 2021, with her January payment reduced by £6,300 and July by £2,100, a total of £8,400. This is because the adjustments made in 2020 save tax at 42% **and** reduce the payments on account for the following year by *the same amount. In cashflow terms, that's a saving of 84%! Sadly, like Vicky, her 'chickens came home to roost' in 2022. Increased profits for the year ended 30th March 2021 meant higher payments on account in 2022, leaving her £4,200 worse off by July that year.*

As with Vicky, by January 2023, Wendy will have paid the same total amount of tax as she always would have done (again her marginal tax rate has never changed). Furthermore, her cashflow advantage was (in broad terms) four times as great and lasted twice as long, so she should be fairly pleased overall. (And, like everyone else, she will be glad of that extra cash in January 2021.)

But, is there any way of stopping the payments on account system getting its revenge at some point? Yes! In fact, I can think of two. Here's the first.

Example 2.2
Let's take the same facts as before except that Wendy's forecast profit share for the year ending 31st March 2022 is only £80,000, the same as was originally forecast for the year ending 31st March 2021 before any accounting adjustments. This will not alter her tax payments in 2021, but her payments in 2022 will now be as follows:

	Before Adjustments	After Adjustments
31st January 2022		
Balancing payment for 2020/21(as before)	£6,380	£14,780
First payment on account for 2021/22	£11,872	£11,872*
	---------	---------
Total tax due	£18,252	£26,652
31st July 2022		
Second payment on account for 2021/22	£11,872	£11,872*
Total tax due over two years:	£59,404	£59,404

* Assuming an appropriate claim to reduce payments on account is made (and using 2020/21 tax rates for her 2021/22 tax forecast)

The second way to maintain your cashflow advantage is to keep making the adjustments, and doing the planning, set out in Chapters 15 to 20, year in, year out. OK, I suppose it may catch up with you when you cease trading, but that could be a very long time away and/or you may have a lower marginal rate by then.

Chapter 24

Accelerating Tax Liabilities to Make Long-Term Savings

In some of the previous chapters, we have discussed the benefits of accelerating taxable income when you currently have a low marginal tax rate and expect it to rise in the next tax year. We have also discussed how this may be relevant to many unincorporated business owners in 2020/21 or 2021/22 (depending on your accounting period).

Obviously, however, accelerating taxable profits, while it may produce long-term savings, may have a detrimental impact on cashflow. Let's look at an example to see how this might work out in practice.

Example
Xenia trades as a fitness instructor, specialising in extreme sports. She has a 31ˢᵗ December accounting date and normally makes annual profits of around £80,000. However, due to the Coronavirus Crisis, she expects her profits for 2020 to plummet to just £25,000, giving her a marginal tax rate of just 29% (see Chapter 13). Nonetheless, in 2021 she expects her profits to rise back to their normal level of £80,000, returning her to a marginal rate of 42% again.

Using some of the techniques in Chapters 15 to 20, Xenia is able to accelerate £15,000 of her taxable profit from 2021 into 2020, giving her a taxable profit of £40,000 for 2020/21 (based on her accounts to 31ˢᵗ December 2020) and £65,000 for 2021/22 (based on her accounts to 31ˢᵗ December 2021). After that she returns to her normal level of £80,000 per year. How does this planning alter her tax payments?

	Before *Planning*	*After* *Planning*
31st January 2021		
Balancing payment for 2019/20	£11,756	£11,756
First payment on account for 2020/21*	£1,947	£4,122
	---------	---------
Total tax due	£13,703	£15,878
31st July 2021		
Second payment on account for 2020/21*	£1,947	£4,122
31st January 2022		
Final liability for 2020/21		
Income Tax	£2,500	£5,500
Class 4 National Insurance	£1,395	£2,745
Class 2 National Insurance	£159	£159
	---------	---------
	£4,054	£8,404
Less:		
Payments on account	£3,894	£8,244
	---------	---------
Balancing payment for 2020/21	£160	£160
First payment on account for 2021/22	£1,947	£4,122
	---------	---------
Total tax due	£2,107	£4,282
31st July 2022		
Second payment on account for 2021/22	£1,947	£4,122
31st January 2023		
Final liability for 2021/22**		
Income Tax	£19,500	£13,500
Class 4 National Insurance	£4,245	£3,945
Class 2 National Insurance	£159	£159
	---------	---------
	£23,904	£17,604
Less:		
Payments on account	£3,894	£8,244
	---------	---------
Balancing payment for 2021/22	£20,010	£9,360
First payment on account for 2022/23	£11,872	£8,722
	---------	---------
Total tax due	£31,882	£18,082
31st July 2023		
Second payment on account for 2022/23	£11,872	£8,722

31st January 2024
*Final liability for 2022/23***

Income Tax	£19,500	£19,500
Class 4 National Insurance	£4,245	£4,245
Class 2 National Insurance	£159	£159
	---------	---------
	£23,904	£23,904
Less:		
Payments on account	£23,744	£17,444
	---------	---------
Balancing payment for 2022/23	£160	£6,460
First payment on account for 2023/24	£11,872	£11,872
	---------	---------
Total tax due	£12,032	£18,332
Total tax due over three years:	£75,490	£73,540

*   *Assuming the appropriate claim to reduce payments on account is made (see Chapter 11)*
**   *Based on 2020/21 tax rates*

In the end, we can see that Xenia has achieved an overall saving of £1,950. This represents the 13% difference in marginal tax rates (42% - 29%) on the income of £15,000 she was able to accelerate.

However, the benefit of this saving took two years to realise (until January 2023) and she suffered higher tax bills in the interim. On the other hand, once the tax saving was achieved there were further cashflow benefits over the next year.

Xenia's **cumulative** cashflow position can be summarised as follows:

	Before	**After**	**Better/(Worse)**
31· January 2021	£13,703	£15,878	(£2,175)
31· July 2021	£15,650	£20,000	(£4,350)
31· January 2022	£17,757	£24,282	(£6,525)
31· July 2022	£19,704	£28,404	(£8,700)
31· January 2023	£51,586	£46,486	£5,100
31· July 2023	£63,458	£55,208	£8,250
31· January 2024	£75,490	£73,540	£1,950

Is It Still Worth It?

If you can spare the funds to meet the higher payments in the first two years then, yes, I would say so.

Even if you ignore the additional positive cashflow achieved in the third year, it's equivalent to investing £2,175 every six months to get a return of £1,950 after two years. That's an average annual rate of return of over 23%.

I'd call that a pretty good investment. It's tax free too!

And you'll get a better rate of return if there's a bigger difference in your marginal tax rates between one year and the next: the change from 29% to 42% that Xenia had is actually one of the smallest.

Chapter 25

VAT Relief on Bad Debts

Many businesses with turnover of less than £1.6m operate the cash accounting scheme (for VAT) and don't account for VAT on their sales until they get paid. Relief for bad debts is therefore automatic.

For those not in the cash accounting scheme, a debt is 'bad' for VAT purposes when it is six months overdue. This means the debt must be unpaid six months after the normal due date. Hence, if you normally give your customers or tenants a month to pay, the debt won't be 'bad' until seven months after an invoice is issued.

At this point, relief can be claimed for the VAT included in the bad debt by adding it to the total in 'Box 4' on the VAT Return as if it were VAT on a purchase.

If some or all of the debt is later recovered, the VAT element of the amount received must then be included in the business's output VAT in 'Box 1' of the VAT Return for the relevant period. The same rate of VAT as was charged on the original sale must be used to calculate the VAT element of any sums recovered.

If you're not in the cash accounting scheme, VAT creates an additional cashflow disadvantage on any bad debts. This may give you cause to hold off invoicing a customer if there appears to be little or no hope of getting paid. If you're on cash accounting though, there is nothing to lose.

Chapter 26

VAT Deregistration

VAT-registered businesses whose annual sales fall below the deregistration threshold of £83,000 may be able to apply to deregister. This may assist cashflow over the next few months, especially for businesses providing services to the general public. However, there are a few hoops to jump through, unfortunately.

When you deregister, HMRC will generally expect you to reduce your gross prices. If not, you will generally need to provide evidence to prove your future turnover (annual sales) will not exceed the deregistration threshold. In other words, they don't really like you deregistering simply because of a temporary reduction in sales (which is what we all hope the current situation will be).

Nonetheless, there will be cases where the Coronavirus Crisis has a permanent, or long-term, impact on a business's annual sales and it will be appropriate to apply for deregistration. Other business owners may take this opportunity to reduce their working hours, or cut out less profitable elements of their business, in the future. Such changes, when combined with the impact of the Coronavirus Crisis, may give you the chance to get that damn VAT monkey off your back by deregistering!

If you do manage to successfully deregister, you will have to account for the VAT previously recovered on goods and assets still on hand at the date your registration is cancelled, unless the amount of this VAT is no more than £1,000.

For this purpose you will need to include all the VAT on goods still in stock, based on their purchase price; but for long-term business assets, such as a computer for example, you only need to include the asset's market value at the date your registration is cancelled.

If you have perishable goods, it may make sense to simply dispose of them before the date your registration is cancelled, especially if you do not expect to sell them in the foreseeable future. (This will not apply to most food, as this is zero rated for VAT, although confectionary is generally standard-rated)

Despite these restrictions, it may still be possible to benefit from VAT deregistration.

Example
Quentin runs a successful hairdressing salon through his company, Kutz Ltd. Some years ago, he had to register the company for VAT because his annual turnover went over the VAT registration threshold. In fact, by February 2020, his annual turnover, including VAT, had reached £120,000.

As a VAT registered business, Kutz Ltd must effectively hand over one sixth of its takings to HMRC each quarter. Hence, for example, if Quentin charges a customer £60 for highlights, then £10 of this represents VAT which the company must pay to HMRC.

Kutz Ltd can, of course, recover the VAT on its supplies, but this is minimal compared with the VAT it has to pay over on its sales.

Due to the Coronavirus Crisis, Quentin had to shut his salon in March 2020. By the end of May, the company's turnover, excluding VAT, for the previous twelve months has fallen to less than £80,000. Furthermore, as he is approaching retirement, Quentin plans to reduce his working hours when the salon reopens, and this is enough to convince HMRC that Kutz Ltd is eligible to deregister.

The company's VAT registration is cancelled from 31st July 2020. In its final VAT return, the company will have to account for VAT previously recovered on goods and assets still on hand in the business at that date.

Knowing he will not reopen until October (he plans to redecorate before reopening), Quentin reviews his stock of hair dyes, shampoo and other products and disposes of anything with a 'use by' date before 15th October. As a result, his stock on hand at 31st July 2020 amounts to only £3,600, meaning there is only £600 of VAT included within it (£4,800 x 20/120 = £600).

His equipment (hairdryers, scissors, etc) cost over £10,000 when new but its market value, second-hand, at 31st July 2020 is no more than £1,800 in total: with the economy in the state it's in at this point, the value of second-hand equipment is very low. Hence, the VAT element in Kutz Ltd's capital assets is just £300 (£1,800 x 20/120), bringing the total VAT on its goods and assets on hand at the date its VAT registration is cancelled to £900, meaning it has no additional VAT to pay in its final VAT return.

When Quentin reopens the salon in October and charges his customer £60 for highlights, the company gets to keep all of it instead of just £50. And all those extra tenners will add up to help Quentin restore his business. He will, however, need to monitor the situation to ensure the company's turnover does not creep back over the VAT deregistration threshold (£83,000). However, his reduced hours mean this shouldn't happen. He used to work an average of 60 hours per week to make £120,000 per year and hand £20,000 in VAT over to HMRC. Now he plans to work 40 hours per week to make £80,000 per year with no VAT to hand over to HMRC. It seems like a much better deal as far as Quentin is concerned.

Note that, if the VAT on Kutz Ltd's goods and assets on hand at 31st July 2020 had exceeded £1,000, it would have had to pay this sum over to HMRC. Let's say instead of £900, as above, it had come to £1,010. In that case, it would have been worthwhile for Quentin to simply give away something worth £60, thus reducing the VAT on the company's goods and assets on hand to £1,000 (which it would not have to pay).

When Not to Deregister

You **must** deregister when you cease trading permanently, but many businesses have only closed temporarily, or are seeing vastly reduced sales, which means their turnover has fallen below the deregistration threshold.

If VAT registration looks to remain sensible for you in the long run, there is no need to deregister just because sales have fallen below the de-registration threshold, and I would tend to advise against deregistration if:

- Your sales are predominantly zero-rated, or subject to the reduced rate of 5%,
- You expect your annual sales to recover to more than £83,000 in the near future, or
- You predominantly make sales to other VAT-registered businesses

Delaying Deregistration During Temporary Closure

If deregistration does look like a good idea, you may wish to delay it and remain registered during the period you are temporarily closed for business. As you are not making any sales, there is no

VAT to account for but, during this period, you will still be able to recover VAT paid on:

- Rent, where appropriate
- Telephone and broadband services
- Electricity supplies and other utilities

You can, of course, also recover VAT on goods you purchase in this period but, as explained above, you would have to pay it back when your registration is cancelled.

Chapter 27

Scottish Taxpayers

Scottish taxpayers pay Income Tax at different rates to those in the rest of the UK. This obviously impacts on marginal rate planning and many other planning issues discussed throughout this guide. We will look at marginal tax rates for Scottish taxpayers later in this chapter. Nonetheless, although the rates of tax paid by Scottish taxpayers may be different, the principles behind all the tax planning discussed in this guide remain the same.

We will look at the question of who is classed as a Scottish taxpayer later in this chapter but, before that, let's look at those Scottish Income Tax rates.

Scottish Income Tax Rates

Scottish taxpayers are entitled to the same personal allowance as other UK resident taxpayers. They are also subject to the withdrawal of that allowance where taxable income exceeds £100,000.

Scottish Income Tax rates **do not** apply to interest, savings and dividend income. Scottish taxpayers pay Income Tax on these types of income at the same rates as other UK taxpayers.

Other crucial points to remember include:

- Scottish taxpayers are subject to the same rates of National Insurance as other UK resident taxpayers
- Scottish taxpayers remain subject to the High Income Child Benefit Charge following the same principles as other taxpayers
- The amount of income, taxable profits, etc, on which a Scottish taxpayer bears tax is computed in exactly the same way as for other UK resident taxpayers: only the rates of tax are different
- Scottish companies are subject to Corporation Tax in exactly the same way as other companies
- Other important taxes are exactly the same in Scotland, including VAT, Inheritance Tax, and Capital Gains Tax

Scottish taxpayers pay Income Tax at the following rates:

Scottish Income Tax Rates with Personal Allowance (PA)

2019/20	2020/21	Tax Rate	
First £12,500	First £12,500	0%	PA
£12,500 to £14,549	£12,500 to £14,585	19%	Starter rate
£14,549 to £24,944	£14,585 to £25,158	20%	Basic rate
£24,944 to £43,430	£25,158 to £43,430	21%	Intermediate rate
£43,430 to £100,000	£43,430 to £100,000	41%	Higher rate
£100,000 to £125,000	£100,000 to £125,000	61.5%	PA withdrawal
£125,000 to £150,000	£125,000 to £150,000	41%	Higher rate
Over £150,000	Over £150,000	46%	Top rate

Combining these with National Insurance at normal UK rates creates the following overall marginal tax rates for Scottish taxpayers:

Scottish Marginal Tax Rates – 2019/20

	Rental/Pension	Self-Emp'd	Employed
First £6,365	0%	0%	0%
£6,365 to £8,632	0%	£156 (1)	0%
£8,632 to £12,500	0%	9%	12%
£12,500 to £14,549	19%	28%	31%
£14,549 to £24,944	20%	29%	32%
£24,944 to £43,430	21%	30%	33%
£43,430 to £50,000	41%	50%	53%
£50,000 to £100,000	41%	43%	43%
£100,000 to £125,000	61.5%	63.5%	63.5%
£125,000 to £150,000	41%	43%	43%
Over £150,000	46%	48%	48%

Scottish Marginal Tax Rates – 2020/21

	Rental/Pension	Self-Emp'd	Employed
First £6,475	0%	0%	0%
£6,475 - £9,500	0%	£159 (2)	0%
£9,500 - £12,500	0%	9%	12%
£12,500 - £14,585	19%	28%	31%
£14,585 - £25,158	20%	29%	32%
£25,158 - £43,430	21%	30%	33%
£43,430 - £50,000	41%	50%	53%
Over £50,000	Same as in 2019/20, as set out above		

Notes
1. Class 2 National Insurance at £3.00 per week
2. Class 2 National Insurance at £3.05 per week
3. Income Tax only rates as per 'Rental/Pension' column also apply to employed or self-employed earners over State Pension Age (approx 66 at present)

Who Is A Scottish Taxpayer?

You are classed as a Scottish taxpayer if you are UK resident and your main place of residence in the UK is in Scotland. Your main place of residence in the UK must be determined as a question of fact, and it is important to remember that, for *this* purpose:

- It is not possible to elect which property is to be treated as your main place of residence
- Only property in the UK is counted
- It is not necessary to have any legal or equitable interest in the property
- Any type of abode may be counted, including hotel rooms and berths on ships and oil rigs
- Each person must be considered individually (i.e. married couples are not treated as a single 'unit')

Hence, while your 'main place of residence' for this purpose will often be the same as your 'main residence' for Capital Gains Tax purposes, the rules are slightly different and may sometimes lead to a different result.

If you move to or from Scotland during the tax year, you will be classified according to where your main place of residence in the UK is for the majority of the year.

If it is not clear whether your main place of residence is located in Scotland for any given tax year then the question of whether you are a Scottish taxpayer for that year will be based on where you have spent the most days. For this purpose, a 'day' is based on where you are at midnight and you become a Scottish taxpayer if you are present in Scotland at midnight on at least as many days as you are present in any of England, Wales, or Northern Ireland (taking each country separately).

Chapter 28

Using the Cash Basis to Save Tax

In Chapters 15 to 20, we focussed on marginal rate planning for unincorporated business owners on traditional 'accruals basis' accounting. However, many small business owners have the option to change to one of the two cash bases now available. As it is possible to join, or leave, the cash bases on a year by year basis (e.g. you could join for 2019/20, leave for 2020/21, join again for 2021/22, etc) this option fits very well with marginal rate planning. More of that later; first, let's look at what changing to a cash basis actually involves.

What's the Difference?

The main difference between traditional 'accruals basis' accounting and the cash basis **is** the **timing** of when income must be recognised and expenses may be deducted.

Under traditional 'accruals basis' accounting, income is recognised when it is earned and expenditure is deducted when it is incurred. Here's a quick example to explain how this works.

Example 1.1
Yvonne is a landlord with a portfolio of residential property. In February 2020 she started renting out a house in London at a monthly rent of £2,500 payable in advance on the first of each month.

Under traditional 'accruals basis' accounting, the rent of £2,500 received on 1st April is only partly taxable in 2019/20, as some of it relates to a period after the year end on 5th April. Hence, instead of £2,500, Yvonne should only include £417 (£2,500 x 5/30) in her accounts for the year ended 5th April 2020.

In early March 2020, Yvonne had some repairs carried out on one of her properties at a cost of £3,200. It was a long time before her builder managed to get around to invoicing her and she didn't pay this bill until August. Nonetheless, under traditional 'accruals basis' accounting, she can deduct the cost of this repairs expenditure in her accounts to 5th April 2020.

As we can see, under traditional 'accruals basis' accounting, Yvonne has been able to make two adjustments that will reduce her taxable profits for 2019/20 by £5,283 (£3,200 + £2,500 − £417). If she's a higher rate taxpayer, this will save her £2,113 in January 2021. If she's also a single mother with two children and would otherwise have had rental profits of £60,000, it will save her £3,058 (see Chapter 44). In fact, if we factor in payments on account, it could save her as much as £3,170 in January 2021 as a 'normal' higher-rate taxpayer; or £4,587 as that single mother of two (but see Chapters 11 and 23 for further analysis of the impact of tax reductions on payments on account).

What Happens under the Cash Basis?

Under the cash basis, income is simply recognised when it is received and expenditure is deductible when it is paid.

This does not alter what income is taxable or, in most cases, what expenditure is deductible, it usually only alters the timing. However, there are a few quirks to be aware of, and some expense deductions may be permanently prohibited under the cash basis. We will explore these issues in detail in Chapters 29 and 31.

The cash bases have the virtue of simplicity and, for this reason they may appeal to small unincorporated business owners. But there are pitfalls to be wary of and, even in a simple case like our example the cash basis could lead to increased tax bills.

Landlords Joining the Cash Basis

In my view, there will generally be an increase in taxable profits for landlords joining the cash basis, although everyone's circumstances are different. Sometimes there are factors that work the other way.

Example 1.2
One of Yvonne's other tenants was in rent arrears at 5th April 2020 and had not paid either their March or February rent of £2,000 per month. They did eventually manage to pay in June, before Yvonne prepares her accounts, so she cannot class this as a 'bad debt' under traditional 'accruals basis' accounting (see Chapter 16). Hence, she would still have to include £2,333 (£2,000 for March plus £2,000 x 5/30 = £333 for April) of rental income from this tenant in her accounts for the year ended 5th April 2020.

On 1st March 2020, Yvonne paid an annual insurance premium on her rental properties of £1,800, covering the period from 6th March 2020 to 5th March 2021. Under traditional 'accruals basis' accounting, she would need to treat 11/12ths of this, or £1,650, as a prepayment and only obtain tax relief for that amount in 2020/21.

We now see that using traditional 'accruals basis' accounting means Yvonne also has to include an extra £3,983 of taxable profit in 2019/20 due to the further timing differences shown in Example 1.2. However, the net position shown by both parts of the example is that using traditional 'accruals basis' accounting means she has £1,300 (£5,283 - £3,983) less rental profit in 2019/20 than she would if she joined the cash basis.

Trading Businesses

Trading businesses differ immensely; they cover a huge range of activities. So, unlike landlords, where we can make some reasonable generalisations, it's hard to say whether joining the cash basis would accelerate or defer taxable profits. Here are a few general pointers though:

- Service businesses (lawyers, graphic designers, architects, etc) – due to the rules on 'work-in-progress' examined in Chapter 18, joining the cash basis will generally defer your taxable profits
- Property developers – as you carry large amounts of trading stock or work-in-progress, the cash basis will generally defer your taxable profits (although such businesses will seldom be eligible to join)
- Retail businesses – due to the need to hold trading stock, the cash basis will generally defer your taxable profits, although this depends on how much credit you take from your suppliers
- Hospitality/leisure – under **normal** circumstances the cash basis would tend to accelerate taxable profits where you are receiving payments in advance for bookings

We will take a closer look at the impact of the cash basis on trading businesses in Chapter 31.

The Cash Bases and Marginal Rate Planning

Whether joining the cash basis accelerates or defers your taxable income, it could have a major role to play in marginal rate planning.

Example 1.3

Let's take the same facts as in Example 1.1 and 1.2 but also throw in the fact that under traditional 'accruals basis' accounting Yvonne could also accrue a further £1,200 for accountancy fees and £500 for other costs. To summarise, the accounting adjustments to her taxable profit under traditional 'accruals basis' accounting are:

Rent received in advance	*- £2,083*
Rent due at accounting date	*+£2,333*
Repairs accrual	*- £3,200*
Accountancy accrual	*- £1,200*
Sundry accruals (but specific)	*- £500*
Insurance prepayment	*+£1,650*

Total	*- £3,000*

In other words, if she joined the cash basis, her taxable profits would increase by £3,000.

However, let us now suppose that, due to the interest relief restrictions discussed in Chapter 21, Yvonne's marginal tax rate will increase from 40% in 2019/20 to 60% in 2020/21. Hence, joining the cash basis for 2019/20 (which she can easily do when she submits her 2020 Tax Return) will mean £3,000 more taxable profit falls into 2019/20 to be taxed at 40% and, if she leaves the cash basis again in 2021/22, £3,000 less will fall into 2021/22 to be taxed at 60%.

This course of action will eventually lead to an ultimate overall saving of £600 (see Chapter 24 regarding the cashflow implications of accelerating taxable profits and an assessment of how worthwhile this may be in the long run).

Note, I have assumed for the sake of illustration that the 'other costs' in Example 1.3 are not interest and finance costs. We will look at how these are treated under the cash basis for landlords in Chapter 29. We'll look at some more examples of marginal rate planning with one of the cash bases in Chapters 29 to 31.

Chapter 29

The Cash Basis for Landlords

The 'cash basis' of accounting is available to 'unincorporated property businesses', i.e. landlords operating as individuals or partnerships. However, it is not available to:

- Businesses with total gross annual rental income exceeding £150,000
- Companies
- Trusts
- LLPs
- Other partnerships with one or more corporate partners

The cash basis is the 'default' option for all eligible landlords. In other words, if you are eligible for the cash basis, it will automatically apply unless you elect to opt out. An election to opt out of the cash basis must be made within one year after the 31st January following the relevant tax year. For example, to elect out of the cash basis for 2019/20, you must make your election by 31st January 2022. The election is made simply by placing an 'X' in Box 5.2 or 20.2, as appropriate, in the UK property supplement of your tax return.

Electing out of the cash basis will ensure you are able to continue using traditional 'accruals basis' accounting and consider all the tax planning measures we examined in Chapters 15 to 20.

For the purposes of both the £150,000 threshold and the question of whether you wish to opt out of the 'cash basis' your UK and overseas properties are regarded as separate businesses. Hence, you could have £100,000 of gross annual rental income from UK property and £100,000 of gross annual rental income from overseas property and still be eligible for the cash basis for both businesses. Furthermore, you could, if you wish, opt out of the cash basis for one of those businesses but remain in the cash basis for the other.

Where you own any rental property jointly with another person, you must both use the same basis (i.e. either the 'cash basis' or traditional 'accruals basis' accounting) for the relevant property business (UK or overseas). This means many landlords with joint interests in property are unable to use the cash basis.

The cash basis closely reflects what many landlords actually do in practice and generally means all rent is taxable when received and allowable expenses may be claimed when paid. Subject to the points below, it does not generally alter the question of which expenses are allowable, only the timing of when they may be claimed. There are some important exceptions to this however.

Disadvantages of the Cash Basis

The cash basis is simpler to operate than the normal accruals basis of accounting, but there are a number of reasons why it will not always be beneficial, including:

i)   Rent becomes fully taxable on receipt, even if it relates to a period that extends beyond the end of the tax year
ii)   Expenses that have been incurred but not yet paid at the end of the tax year cannot be claimed
iii)   There is a potential further restriction on interest relief (in addition to the measures discussed in Chapter 21), although this can only arise where borrowings exceed the original cost of rental properties and will not affect many landlords in practice – see the Taxcafe.co.uk guide *How to Save Property Tax* for full details
iv)   Abortive expenditure relating to potential purchases of new property that are abandoned will not be allowable
v)   Costs of raising loan finance incurred in earlier years and which were being claimed over the useful life of the loan (see the Taxcafe.co.uk guide *How to Save Property Tax* for details) cannot be claimed
vi)   No deductions are allowed for lease premiums paid

Example 1
Zoe is a higher-rate taxpayer with a salary of £60,000. During 2019/20, she also received rent totalling £120,000, incurred interest costs of £70,000, and other expenses of £20,000, including £1,000 for some surveys on properties she later decided not to buy and £5,000 for some roof repairs carried out in February 2020 which she paid in May. £12,000 of Zoe's income was received in the first five days of April 2020 and relates to the rent due for the whole of that month. £4,000 of her interest costs represents an accrual for costs arising to 5th April but paid later.

146

Zoe's accountant works out her profit under traditional 'accruals basis' accounting principles:

Income due for the year	*£110,000*
(£120,000 - £12,000 x 25/30)	
Less expenses:	
Interest	*£70,000*
Other expenses incurred	*£20,000*
Accrued accountancy fees	*£2,000*

Rental profit	*£18,000*

(As explained in Chapter 21, £52,500, or 75%, of Zoe's interest expense will be added back to profit for tax purposes and will instead give rise to a tax deduction at basic rate)

If Zoe does not elect to use traditional 'accruals basis' accounting, she will fall into the cash basis by default and her profit will then be calculated as follows:

Income received in the year	*£120,000*
Less expenses paid in the year:	
Interest (£70,000 - £4,000)	*£66,000*
Other	*£14,000*
(£15,000 paid less survey costs not allowed £1,000)	
Net rental income	*£40,000*

(£49,500, or 75%, of Zoe's allowable interest will be added to her income for tax purposes and will instead give rise to a tax deduction at basic rate)

The cash basis would therefore cause a considerable increase in Zoe's tax liability. Her taxable profit would be increased by £19,000, from £70,500 (£18,000 + £52,500) to £89,500 (£40,000 + £49,500); and her interest costs allowed for basic rate relief purposes would be reduced by £1,000, from £17,500 (£70,000 x 25%) to £16,500 (£66,000 x 25%)

Her tax liability in January 2021 will have increased by £7,800 (£19,000 x 40% + £1,000 x 20%) – ignoring payments on account for the sake of illustration.

It must be admitted that much of the difference arising in Zoe's case is only a question of timing. Nonetheless, she has also permanently lost out on £1,000 worth of allowable expenses (the abortive survey costs) and a further £4,000 (her accrued interest costs) has been pushed from a period where 25% of it is still allowable as a deduction into a period where all of it provides basic rate relief only.

And timing is nothing to be sniffed at. Apart from the permanent loss of allowable expenses and deferral of interest relief, a further £17,000 of taxable income has arisen at least a year earlier. For a higher rate taxpayer, that alone means paying £6,800 in tax at least a year earlier, so it's not exactly unimportant.

Advantages of the Cash Basis

In addition to the fact that it is simpler to operate, the cash basis does have some other potential advantages. Many of these again relate to timing. In this context, it is worth remembering that many landlords who were basic rate taxpayers up to 2019/20 could become higher rate taxpayers in 2020/21 as a result of the restrictions to interest relief discussed in Chapter 21. We looked at an example of a landlord whose marginal tax rate was increasing in Chapter 28 and while in that case her marginal rate increased from 40% to 60%, the principles (and potential savings) are the same when it is increasing from 20% to 40%.

However, as we saw in Chapter 21, there are many conflicting factors to consider for landlords at the moment and other landlords may suffer a significant drop in taxable income in 2020/21 as a result of the Coronavirus Crisis, despite the restrictions in interest relief. Some landlords may see voids, causing significant reductions in their taxable profits, and meaning they have a lower marginal tax rate in 2020/21 than they would expect to have in 2021/22. In these cases, it may be worth joining the cash basis and thus perhaps accelerating some taxable income from 2021/22 into 2020/21, where it will be taxed at a lower rate.

Example 2
Akiko is a residential landlord with no other sources of income. In 2020/21, she suffers a number of voids with the result that her rental income received in the year falls from £87,000 in 2019/20 to just £48,000 in 2020/21. This makes her a basic rate taxpayer for 2020/21, although things recover in 2021/22, making her a higher-rate taxpayer again. She has previously managed to pay off her buy-to-let mortgages

so she does not incur any interest and finance costs.

On both 1st April 2019 and 1st April 2021, Akiko receives £7,500 in rent which relates to the month of April. Her accountant Billie adjusts this by treating £6,250 as 'receipts in advance' which can be deferred into the next tax year. However, in 2020, while £7,500 was due on 1st April as usual, Akiko only received £4,500, although the rest was paid later. Billie thus treats 25/30ths of £4,500 as 'receipts in advance' and includes 5/30ths of the amount unpaid (£3,000) as 'rent due but unpaid'.

Billie also puts in an accrual for his own fees, which amount to £1,200 (including VAT) each year. He accrues other costs where necessary and puts through an adjustment in respect of Akiko's annual insurance premium which is due on 1st July each year in respect of the year to the following 30th June (see Chapter 19).

During the voids, Akiko took the opportunity to do some discretionary repairs expenditure, including replacing the bathrooms in two of her properties at a cost of £10,000 (this was simply 'modernisation' with no improvement element, so this represents allowable repairs expenditure). The builder agreed to allow her to pay for this in instalments and she still owes £6,000 at 5th April 2021.

The voids also led to some additional costs for Akiko: she had to pay £1,000 in various standing charges (gas, electricity, etc) on her empty properties and owes the council £2,000 in Council Tax, which she is disputing.

When Billie prepares Akiko's letting statement under traditional 'accruals basis' accounting principles, it looks as follows (he always includes last year for comparative purposes because he's a good accountant, a member of the ICAEW, in fact):

	2019/20	2020/21
Rental income received	£87,000	£48,000
Add opening receipts in advance	£6,250	£3,750
Add rent due, not yet paid	£500	
Less closing receipts in advance	(£3,750)	(£6,250)
Less opening rent due		(£500)
	---------	----------
Rental income taxable in the year	£90,000	£45,000

Less:
Repairs and maintenance

	2019/20	2020/21
Expenditure in year	£2,500	£8,000
Closing creditor		£6,000
Insurance		
Opening prepayment	£600	£640
Premium paid	£2,560	£2,800
Closing prepayment	(£640)	(£700)
Accountancy fees	£1,200	£1,200
Utilities		£1,000
Council Tax		£2,000
Legal fees accrual		£750*
Sundry allowable expenses		
Opening accruals	(£250)	(£140)
Amounts paid	£1,000	£800
Closing accruals	£140	£325
	---------	----------
Total expenditure	£7,110	£22,675
	---------	----------
Rental profits	£82,890	£22,325

* - Billie's estimate of costs relating to the Council Tax dispute

However, Billie also points out to Akiko that she has an opportunity to make some significant long-term tax savings by joining the cash basis for 2020/21. This will accelerate part of her taxable profits for 2021/22 into 2020/21, producing an overall saving equal to 20% of the amount taxed in the earlier year. "How much could I save?" she asks. "I'll show you," he says, and produces her tax calculation for 2020/21, prepared on a cash basis, as follows:

Rental income received	£48,000
Add opening receipts in advance	£3,750
Less opening rent due	(£500)

Rental income taxable in the year	£51,250
Less:	
Repairs and maintenance	
Expenditure in year	£8,000
Insurance	
Opening prepayment	£640
Premium paid	£2,800
Accountancy fees	
Opening accrual	(£1,200)
Amount paid	£1,200
Utilities	£1,000
Sundry allowable expenses	
Opening accruals	(£140)
Amounts paid	£800

Total expenditure	£13,100

Rental profits	£38,150

Joining the cash basis will increase Akiko's taxable profits for 2019/20 by £15,825 (£38,150 - £22,325) BUT all of this increase will reverse in 2020/21 if she then leaves the cash basis and returns to traditional 'accruals basis' accounting. Hence, while she'll pay an extra £3,165 in basic rate tax at 20% for 2019/20, she will save £6,330 in higher rate tax for 2020/21, leaving her £3,165 better off overall.

See Chapter 24 regarding the cashflow implications of this strategy, including an analysis of how valuable it is as an 'investment'.

Note that, due to the transitional rules explained below, the opening adjustments (e.g. 'opening receipts in advance', 'opening accruals', etc) must still be made in the year the landlord joins the cash basis. However, the good news is that those same transitional rules also ensure the amount of profit effectively accelerated into the year the landlord joins the cash basis is effectively deducted in the year they leave the cash basis and return to traditional 'accruals basis' accounting.

Entering or Leaving the Cash Basis

Transitional rules apply in the year a landlord joins or leaves the cash basis. In effect, these rules ensure:

- No income escapes tax
- No income is taxed twice
- Expenses cannot be claimed twice

Generally, the transitional rules should also ensure allowable expenses are not omitted, but this is subject to the points listed under 'Disadvantages of the Cash Basis' above. Example 2 above provides a good illustration of the transitional rules in action.

Capital Expenditure under the Cash Basis

Landlords operating the cash basis may generally claim capital expenditure as it is paid; provided it would otherwise qualify for capital allowances or replacement of domestic items relief (see the Taxcafe.co.uk guide *How to Save Property Tax*). Certain expenditure cannot be claimed under the cash basis, however, including cars, land and buildings, 'integral features' and the other excluded items listed in Chapter 31.

With the exception of cars (see below) and expenditure relating to the other excluded items listed in Chapter 31, brought forward balances in capital allowances pools are claimed in full in the year the landlord enters the cash basis. This represents a further advantage of entering the cash basis, but will seldom be of any great benefit as most landlords will already have claimed all their eligible expenditure in previous years under the Annual Investment Allowance.

Landlords using the cash basis should continue to claim capital allowances on cars under the usual principles. Apart from cars, landlords using the cash basis may not claim any other capital allowances.

Summary

In general, under *normal* circumstances, my view is that the cash basis will not usually be beneficial for most landlords for the simple reason that rent is usually received in advance and many expenses are paid in arrears. Hence, the cash basis will generally have the effect of accelerating taxable income into an earlier year.

However, between the Coronavirus Crisis and the Government's diabolical restrictions on interest relief, ***these are not normal times*** and the ***cash basis for landlords now represents a useful tool*** to be implemented in marginal rate planning, potentially saving many landlords thousands of pounds.

Nonetheless, when things do get back to normal, I would expect most landlords to be better off sticking with, or returning to, traditional 'accruals basis' accounting – BUT, even then, it will always be worth considering whether the cash basis might be beneficial when the landlord is eligible.

Chapter 30

Using the Cash Basis to Help With Rent Arrears

An additional point to consider with the cash basis is the question of how much it might assist landlords suffering rent arrears during the Coronavirus Crisis. To examine this question, let's return to Example 1 in Chapter 29 and take the landlord forward in time by a year.

Example Resumed

Zoe opted out of the cash basis in 2019/20, but her circumstances have changed a lot in 2020/21. She remains a higher-rate taxpayer, as she continues to receive a salary of £60,000 but, out of the £144,000 rent she should have received, she had only received £59,000 by 5th April 2021, although thankfully all but £15,000 of the arrears have been paid by the time she is preparing her 2020/21 accounts.

She paid interest of £56,000 in 2020/21, with another £3,200 accrued but unpaid as at 5th April 2021. Repairs expenditure this year has been minimal, although she did, of course, pay the £5,000 for the roof repairs carried out last year.

Her actual accountancy fees for 2019/20 turned out to be £2,500, which she paid in January 2021, and the accrued fees for 2020/21 amount to £2,800 (she's been talking to her friend Akiko about possibly moving her business to Akiko's accountant, who seems to be much better value).

Other expenditure includes an insurance premium of £3,600 paid in December 2020 to cover the year commencing 1st January 2021. Zoe remembers this well as she was infuriated by the dramatic increase from last year's premium of £2,700.

When Zoe's accountant tells her she will have a tax bill of over £30,000 to pay in January 2022, she turns to Akiko, who suggests she might want to consider the cash basis. After being prompted by Zoe, her accountant comes up with the following comparison:

	Accruals Basis	**Cash Basis**
Rental income received	£59,000	£59,000
Add opening receipts in advance*	£10,000	£10,000
Add rent due, not yet paid	£85,000	
Less closing receipts in advance**	(£10,000)	
	----------	----------
Rental income taxable in the year	£144,000	£69,000
Less:		
Bad debt provision		
(specific: see Chapter 16)	£15,000	
Repairs and maintenance		
Opening accrual*	(£5,000)	(£5,000)
Expenditure in year	£6,500	£6,500
Insurance		
Opening prepayment	£2,025	£2,025
Premium paid	£3,600	£3,600
Closing prepayment	(£2,700)	
Accountancy fees		
Opening accrual*	(£2,000)	(£2,000)
Paid in year	£2,500	£2,500
Closing accrual	£2,800	
Sundry other allowable expenses	£8,000	£8,000
	----------	----------
Total expenditure	£30,725	£15,625
	----------	----------
Taxable rental profits	£113,275	£53,375
Interest relieved at basic rate		
Opening accrual*	(£4,000)	(£4,000)
Paid in year	£56,000	£56,000
Closing accrual	£3,200	
	----------	----------
	£55,200	£52,000

Income Tax Calculation 2020/21
(NB: £60,000 salary is taxed first: see Chapter 13)

Taxable rental profits

£90,000/£56,375 @ 40%	£36,000	£22,550
£23,275 @ 45%	£10,474	
Personal allowance withdrawal		
£12,500/£6,687*** @ 40%	£5,000	£2,675
	---------	----------
	£51,474	£25,225
Less:		
Basic rate tax relief on interest costs		
£55,200/£52,000 @ 20%	£11,040	£10,400
	---------	----------
Final tax liability for 2020/21	£40,434	£14,825
Less:		
Payments on account****	£29,700	£29,700
	---------	----------
Balancing payment/(repayment)		
for 2020/21	£10,374	(£14,875)
First payment on account		
for 2021/22	£20,217	£7,412
	---------	----------
Tax payment/(repayment)		
due 31· January 2022	£30,591	(£7,463)

*   *See Example 1 in Chapter 29*
**   *£144,000/12 - £12,000 per month x 25/30 = £10,000 (same as in 2020 per Example 1 in Chapter 29)*
***   *£60,000 + £53,375 - £100,000 = £13,375/2 = £6,687 – see Chapter 13 for explanation*
****   *Based on 2019/20 results under traditional 'accruals basis' accounting, as per Example 1 in Chapter 29*

By moving to the cash basis, Zoe saves £25,609 (£40,434 - £14,825) on her tax liability for 2020/21. Furthermore, she eliminates a tax bill of over £30,000 in January 2022, and gets a repayment of £7,463 instead, a cashflow saving of £38,054 (£30,591 + £7,463), with a further saving of £12,805 (£20,217 - £7,412) in July, by which point she is £50,859, **more than £50,000, better off** in total.

How much of this is an absolute, permanent, saving and how much is a cashflow saving will depend on Zoe's results in later years but, right now, who cares: she's got more than £50,000 extra cash to help her recover from the difficulties she went through in 2020/21.

Furthermore, if she'd been able to anticipate her move to the cash basis sooner, she could have reduced her payments on account in January and July 2021 (see Chapter 11), achieving some of her cashflow savings sooner.

Somehow, I suspect, she might sack her accountant and move to Billie (see Chapter 29).

Chapter 31

The Cash Basis for Trading Businesses

Individuals and partnerships with small trading businesses can elect to be taxed under the 'cash basis' (also known as 'cash accounting'). This cash accounting is not to be confused with the VAT scheme also called cash accounting!

The cash basis is generally only available where the annual turnover (i.e. sales) of the business does not exceed £150,000. Those who are already using the cash basis may continue to do so, provided their turnover does not exceed £300,000.

Subject to a number of restrictions, adjustments, etc, (as we will see below) businesses electing to use the cash basis are taxed on the difference between business income received during the year and qualifying business expenses paid during the year, instead of under traditional 'accruals basis' accounting principles.

Capital Expenditure

Where the 'cash basis' is used, qualifying capital expenditure may simply be claimed as it is paid. However, while many of the items that are typically purchased by a small business will qualify, there are some detailed rules that prohibit a great deal of other expenditure from qualifying. Capital expenditure may only be claimed under the 'cash basis' if it meets these detailed rules. The following items of capital expenditure cannot be claimed:

i)   Cars. Motor expenses must continue to be claimed under one of the two alternative methods already available (see the Taxcafe.co.uk guide *'Small Business Tax Saving Tactics'*) including capital allowances where appropriate (i.e. where fixed mileage rates are not being claimed).

ii)   Land and buildings. This includes the cost of 'integral features', and other fixtures that might normally qualify for capital allowances, where these are purchased as part of the purchase of business premises. Additional fixtures added to a building later may, however, qualify and replacements will, of course, usually be correctly classed as repairs and not as capital expenditure.

For example, where a light fitting is purchased as part of the cost of the building, the cost cannot be claimed but, where an additional new light fitting is added later, this can be claimed under the cash basis.

iii) Acquisition and disposal costs (the costs of buying or selling the business, or part of the business).

iv) Education and training. HMRC regards any costs incurred to train a business owner (sole trader or partner) in a new field of expertise as 'personal capital expenditure' that cannot be claimed for Income Tax purposes. This applies equally under traditional 'accruals basis' accounting principles so this provision simply confirms this also applies under the cash basis.

Expenditure on updating or expanding a business owner's knowledge within an existing field of expertise remains allowable (where relevant to the business) and expenditure on training employees is unaffected.

v) Non-depreciating assets. Assets with an expected useful life of 20 years or more, and which will retain at least 10% of their initial value after 20 years, do not qualify.

vi) Assets not acquired for continuing use in the business. This is another rule that would apply equally under traditional 'accruals basis' accounting principles.

vii) Financial assets. This covers obvious items such as stocks and shares or offshore bonds, as well as other types of financial instrument.

viii) Intangible assets. The cost of intangible assets cannot be claimed unless they have a fixed life of less than 20 years. This includes any form of intellectual property, such as patents, trademarks or copyright. Note, however, that most expenditure on software is actually just a licence to use the software, so this would not be prevented from qualifying by this rule.

Costs incurred in connection with the purchase or sale of any of these items (e.g. legal fees, brokers fees, Stamp Duty, etc) are also prohibited. This exclusion is extended to the costs of any abortive, or unsuccessful, attempts to buy or sell any of these items. HMRC has long maintained that such 'abortive' costs are also disallowable under traditional 'accruals basis' accounting principles. While this view may be appropriate in some circumstances, they tend to take something of a 'blanket' view on this issue and this approach is not always correct. What the cash basis legislation does therefore, is to ensure their blanket view always applies.

The cost of vans or motor cycles may be claimed under the cash basis, but if the purchase cost is claimed in this way, mileage allowances will not be available and an appropriate proportion of actual costs must be claimed instead.

Premiums paid to take out a lease on business premises would be excluded under heading (ii) above. Under traditional 'accruals basis' accounting rules, part of the premium could usually be claimed for Income Tax purposes (for example, 92% of the premium paid for a five year lease could be claimed over the life of that lease). Those using the cash basis might therefore be better off negotiating a higher level of rent instead.

Finally, remember the above restrictions only apply to capital expenditure. They do not apply to other valid business expenditure, such as the cost of trading stock, repairs and maintenance, or licence fees.

Previous Capital Expenditure

Where a business entering the cash basis has unrelieved expenditure brought forward from the previous accounting period in its capital allowances pools that balance becomes fully deductible in the first year the business is on the cash basis. This deduction is subject to a few restrictions, however:

- Any applicable reduction to reflect an element of private use must be applied in the same was as for capital allowances
- Any element of expenditure remaining within the pool balance, that would not have qualified under the detailed restrictions set out under headings (i) to (viii) above, cannot be claimed

160

- Any element of the pool balance that has not yet actually been paid cannot be claimed. This will restrict claims on assets purchased under HP or other credit terms

Naturally, it follows from the second restriction that any element of expenditure relating to a car cannot be claimed in this way and only writing down allowances may be claimed as usual. Other items may also be affected but, in these cases, no writing down allowances will be available unless, and until, the business reverts to traditional 'accruals basis' accounting.

Where the third restriction applies, future payments will generally qualify for relief under the 'cash basis' as and when paid.

The main pitfall to watch out for, however, is that, where the unpaid balance on any previous capital expenditure is actually greater than the balance of unrelieved expenditure on the capital allowances pool, the excess will be treated as additional taxable income in the first tax year the business uses the cash basis, thus leading to an additional tax charge.

At first glance, the ability to claim the entire balance of unrelieved expenditure on the business's capital allowances pools looks like a good reason to join the cash basis. However, due to the annual investment allowance, most small businesses now have little or no balance of unrelieved expenditure in their capital allowances pools. Hence, there will be little benefit to be gained by joining the cash basis and, worse still, many may be caught out by the charge arising in respect of unpaid balances on HP contracts, etc.

A Simple Idea?

The basic idea is simple enough. Under the cash accounting method, income is taxable when it is received and expenditure is deductible when it is paid. So, in effect, the theory is there is no need to worry about debtors, creditors, accruals, prepayments, or stock valuations.

The additional benefit (in theory) is that expenditure on equipment, machinery, and most other items will be allowed when it is paid, with no need to distinguish between 'revenue' and 'capital' expenditure (subject to the restrictions examined above).

All these things are just a matter of timing, so the idea is the business will be no better or worse off in the end, even though the amount of profit that is taxed in any given year may change.

But timing is SO important! Most business owners are much more concerned about how much tax they will have to pay this year than whether they are going to pay the same amount of tax between now and when they sell up!

The First Red Herring

Cash accounting is available to sole traders and partnerships with annual sales not exceeding £150,000. It is not available to companies, Limited Liability Partnerships, or other partnerships not composed entirely of individuals.

So, the first red herring to highlight is the so-called benefit of not needing to distinguish between 'revenue' and 'capital' expenditure. Businesses can normally claim an immediate 100% deduction on up to £200,000 of capital expenditure each year (£1m for the two years from 1st January 2019 to 31st December 2020: see Chapter 6). This is plenty enough to cover most expenditure by businesses with annual sales of no more than £150,000.

Furthermore, the idea that capital expenditure is simpler under cash accounting has been 'blown out of the water' by the restrictions we examined above!

Hence, as far as capital expenditure is concerned, very few small businesses would see any advantage if they used cash accounting and many will suffer from the additional disallowances discussed earlier.

For Better or Worse?

Under ***normal*** circumstances, the way to assess whether cash accounting might be beneficial for your business is to start by considering what the impact on the timing of your business profits is likely to be. In other words, will profits generally be accelerated and taxed earlier, or will they generally be deferred and taxed later?

Under cash accounting, you will not be taxed on your debtors (sales you have made but not yet been paid for). You will also be able to claim a full deduction for expenses you have paid, without any adjustments for closing stock or prepayments (see Chapters 17 to 19).

However, you will not be able to claim a deduction for business creditors (purchases made but not paid yet) or accruals (expenses that relate to the period of trading, but which will arise later).

Example 1.1

Claudia opened a new fashion retail shop on 6th April 2019. In the year to 5th April 2020, she took £60,000 in sales and made the following expense payments:

Rent	*£13,000*
Electricity	*£2,000*
Equipment	*£4,000*
Insurance	*£2,000*
Stock purchases	*£20,000*

If Claudia uses the cash accounting method, she will have a 'profit' for tax purposes of £19,000.

Under traditional 'accruals basis' accounting, however, Claudia would have a few adjustments to make. Firstly, she would not claim her equipment purchases as an expense but would instead claim capital allowances of the same amount – hence the 'red herring' referred to above, as there is no overall effect on her taxable profits.

Next, Claudia would need to reduce her expense claims for:

Prepaid rent for 6th to 30th April 2020 - £833
Prepaid insurance relating to period post-5th April 2020 - £500
Stock on hand at 5th April 2020 - £4,000

However, she would also increase her expense claims for:

Unpaid electricity bill - £500
Trade creditors (goods purchased not yet paid for) - £6,000
Accountancy fee accrual - £1,500

Finally, she would also reduce her sales to take account of goods returned after 5th April 2020, £333.

These adjustments would reduce her overall taxable profit to £16,000, saving her at least £870 in Income Tax and National Insurance.

As we can see, Claudia would be worse off under the cash accounting method in her first year of trading since she would be taxed on a higher business profit.

I am not for a second suggesting this would always be the case. It happened in Claudia's case mainly because her business creditors and expense accruals were greater than her business debtors, closing stock value and expense prepayments.

And this is the comparison every business owner needs to make in order to initially determine whether cash accounting might be beneficial for them under normal circumstances. In short, it will generally come down to a question of whether debtors and stock (current assets) tend to be greater than creditors and accruals (current liabilities).

At this stage, it is worth pointing out that this is often where a good accountant proves their worth, by making the adjustments that correctly reflect all the true costs of the trading period, thus reducing the value of current assets and making sure all the relevant liabilities are taken into account. This, in turn, brings the trading profits down to the correct level – but the scope to do this is lost under the cash accounting method.

Nonetheless, even after these adjustments, there will be some businesses where the comparison made above will go the opposite way to Claudia's and these businesses might benefit from cash accounting – but only 'might': because there are a few additional problems to be considered!

Cash Accounting Restrictions

Any business adopting cash accounting is limited to a maximum annual claim of £500 for interest on cash borrowings (business loans and overdrafts) and other associated costs such as loan arrangement fees. Other interest costs, such as hire purchase interest, mortgage interest on business premises, and credit card interest on purchases of business assets will generally be allowable in full.

Well that's simple isn't it? Buy a piece of equipment on HP and you get the interest allowed; take out a bank loan to buy it and you may be denied any relief for the interest. Really simple, yeah!

Example 1.2

Claudia took out a five-year loan of £20,000 to get her business started. She paid a loan arrangement fee of £500. She also has a business overdraft facility of £5,000 for which she paid a fee of £90. During the year to 5ᵗʰ April 2020, she incurred £300 in interest on her overdraft and £1,200 on her loan. Under traditional 'accruals basis' accounting, Claudia may claim the following deductions for these items:

Loan arrangement fee (1/5th)	*£100*
Overdraft fee	*£90*
Interest (£300 + £1,200)	*£1,500*
Total:	*£1,690*

These reduce her taxable profit for the year to 5ᵗʰ April 2020 to £14,310 (£16,000 - £1,690).

Under cash accounting, she is restricted to a claim of just £500 to cover these items. This leaves her with a taxable profit of £18,500 (£19,000 - £500), £4,190 more than under traditional 'accruals basis' accounting. This would probably cost her at least £1,215 in additional Income Tax and National Insurance. Furthermore, the differences relating to interest and finance costs are not just a matter of timing: these are permanent restrictions in Claudia's deductible expenditure.

On the plus side, it is worth noting that a deduction of up to £500 may still be claimed where the business owner incurs interest costs that are only partly for business purposes.

For example, if interest of £1,000 were incurred on a bank loan taken out to finance the purchase of equipment used only 25% for business purposes, traditional 'accruals basis' accounting principles would restrict the deductible expense to just £250 but a business owner using cash accounting could claim £500.

Nonetheless, the total deduction for all interest and finance costs on cash borrowings is still restricted to just £500 per year.

Cash Accounting Losses

'Negative' results (i.e. losses) arising under cash accounting are only available to carry forward for relief against future profits from the same trade. This means that business owners cannot claim relief for trading losses against other income arising in the same year or the previous one, or even against the previous year's profits from the same trade. New business owners will also be denied the opportunity to carry losses back for relief against other income in the previous three years (see Chapter 36).

Marginal Rate Planning with Cash Accounting

Despite all the drawbacks to cash accounting for trading businesses, it remains a valuable tool in marginal rate planning:

Example 2

Denise runs a small cafe and draws up accounts to 31ˢᵗ December each year. At 31ˢᵗ December 2019, she had a booming business and her profits for the year, calculated under traditional 'accruals basis' accounting were £60,000, making her a higher-rate taxpayer with a marginal tax rate of 42% (see Chapter 13). This was after taking account of the following current liabilities:

Trade creditors	*£2,500 (Suppliers awaiting payment)*
Accruals	*£1,500 (Utilities, accountancy fees, etc)*

And the following current assets

Trade debtors	*£500 (A few customers she allows credit)*
Prepayments	*£1,900 (Insurance, rent, etc)*
Trading stock	*£7,500 (Stocks of food, drinks, etc)*

The net effect of all these adjustments was to increase Denise's trading profit by £5,900. However, these adjustments are just a matter of timing. She also pays interest of £1,250 on a business loan, and would see this deduction reduced to just £500 if she were to join the cash basis. This would represent the permanent loss of £750 of deductible expenditure, costing her an extra £315 in tax she would never recoup.

However, due to the Coronavirus Crisis, Denise's profits for the year ended 31ˢᵗ December 2020, computed under traditional 'accruals basis' accounting, are just £10,000, giving her a marginal tax rate of just 9% (see Chapter 13). Her tax for 2019/20 and 2020/21, computed under traditional 'accruals basis' accounting can be summarised as follows:

	2019/20	2020/21
Taxable profit*	£60,000	£10,000
Income Tax @ 20% on profits from £12,500 to £50,000	£7,500	-
Income Tax @ 40% on profits over £50,000	£4,000	-
Class 4 National Insurance @ 9% (see Chapter 10)	£3,723	£45
Class 4 National Insurance @ 2% (see Chapter 10)	£200	-
Class 2 National Insurance	£156	£159
	----------	--------
Tax due for the year	£15,579	£204

* Based on results for accounting period ending during tax year (see Chapter 10)

Due to her dire results in 2020/21, Denise decides to join the cash basis for 2019/20 then leave it and revert to traditional 'accruals basis' accounting, for 2020/21. Due to the transitional rules (broadly the same as those we examined in Chapter 29), this alters her taxable profits and tax liabilities as follows:

	2019/20	2020/21
Taxable profit under accruals basis	£60,000	£10,000
Adjust for items not yet paid at 5 April 2020:		
Trade creditors	£2,500	(£2,500)
Accruals	£1,500	(£1,500)
Sales income not yet received at 5 April 2020:		
Trade debtors	(£500)	£500
Items paid at 5 April 2020:		
Prepayments	(£1,900)	£1,900
Trading stock	(£7,500)	£7,500
Interest disallowed (as above)	£750	
	----------	---------
Revised taxable profit	£54,850	£15,900
Income Tax @ 20% on profits from £12,500 to £50,000	£7,500	£680
Income Tax @ 40% on profits over £50,000	£1,940	-
Class 4 National Insurance @ 9% (see Chapter 10)	£3,723	£576
Class 4 National Insurance @ 2% (see Chapter 10)	£97	-
Class 2 National Insurance	£156	£159
	----------	---------
Tax due for the year	£13,416	£1,415

By following this strategy, Denise has reduced her total tax bill for the two tax years from £15,783 (£15,579 + £204) to £14,831 (£13,416 + £1,415), a saving of £952.

Although she suffered a permanent loss of tax relief on £750 worth of interest, costing her an extra £315, this was outweighed by moving £5,900 worth of profit from a marginal rate of 42%, to

£2,500 taxed at just 9%, thus saving £2,500 x 33% £825
£3,400 taxed at 29%, thus saving £2,200 x 13%   £442

Chapter 32

Is Now a Good Time to Incorporate?

Transferring an unincorporated business into your own company is known as 'incorporation' and is often a good tax planning or business strategy in its own right.

There are a number of reasons why now might be a good time to incorporate.

Property Values

When you transfer property into your own company, the basic rule for both Capital Gains Tax and Stamp Duty Land Tax (or its equivalents in Scotland and Wales) is that the transfer is treated like a sale at market value. Hence you, the transferor, are subject to Capital Gains Tax; and the company, the transferee, is subject to Stamp Duty Land Tax (or its equivalents). Taken together, that can be a pretty hefty tax charge, presenting a major barrier to many business incorporations.

However, a number of reliefs are available, especially for Capital Gains Tax. Your own trading premises; furnished holiday lets; and property letting businesses where you, the owner, spend more than 20 hours per week working in the business (on average) can all be transferred free of Capital Gains Tax under 'incorporation relief'. Alternatively, trading premises and furnished holiday lets also qualify for holdover relief.

Partnership property can also generally be transferred into a company run by the same individuals who are currently the business partners free from Stamp Duty Land Tax (or its equivalents).

Full details of all these valuable reliefs are given in the Taxcafe.co.uk guide *Using a Property Company to Save Tax*.

However, despite these reliefs many business incorporations could give rise to substantial Stamp Duty Land Tax costs and some (e.g. a property letting business that doesn't qualify as furnished holiday let and which you spend less than 20 hours per week working on) could give rise to substantial Capital Gains Tax costs as well.

Hence, with property values falling as a result of the Coronavirus Crisis, this may be a good time to transfer business property into your own company.

Example
Jennifer has wanted to transfer her trading premises into her own company for years. She can avoid Capital Gains Tax on the transfer by claiming holdover relief but has always been put off by the Stamp Duty Land Tax cost. In February 2020, the property was worth £800,000 and the Stamp Duty Land Tax arising on a transfer would have been £29,500*. However, by June, the property's value had fallen to £600,000. Jennifer seizes her chance and makes the transfer. The Stamp Duty Land Tax arising is now reduced to £19,500*, saving Jennifer £10,000.

* - The Stamp Duty Land Tax Rates on Non-Residential Property are:

Up to £150,000	0%
£150,000 to £250,000	2%
Over £250,000	5%

Terminal Loss Relief

If your trading business is making losses, incorporating the business may be a good way to get bigger tax repayments. Normally, losses can only be carried back as far as the previous tax year. However, as explained in Chapter 36, when a trading business ceases, losses arising in the last twelve months of the trade may be carried back against income in the final tax year of the trade and the previous three tax years. For this purpose, transferring the trade into the company is treated the same as ceasing to trade.

Example
Kim has traded successfully for many years, recording the following results:

Year ended 31ˢᵗ March 2018: profit of £120,000
Year ended 31ˢᵗ March 2019: profit of £140,000
Year ended 31ˢᵗ March 2020: profit of £85,000

However, in the period from April to September 2020, he makes a loss of £250,000. He expects to recoup some of this over the next few months, but would still expect a loss of around £210,000 for the year ending 31st March 2021.

As things stand, Kim can only carry back losses of £85,000, to give him a tax saving of £25,923 for 2019/20 (Income Tax and Class 4 National Insurance), leaving the rest of his anticipated losses for the year ending 31st March 2021 to be carried forward for relief at an unknown future date.

Instead, however, he decides to incorporate his business on 1st October 2020 and is therefore able to claim terminal loss relief for losses arising in the last twelve months of trading. The tax relief 'cap' (see Chapter 40) does not apply as he will be setting his losses off against profits from the same trade.

For terminal loss relief purposes, losses arising in the last twelve months of trading are calculated on a strict tax year basis. Unless you incorporate (or cease trading) on 5th April, your last twelve months of trading will span two tax years. Each must be considered separately and if either gives rise to a profit, this will be ignored in the calculation of your terminal losses. Kim's terminal losses are therefore calculated as follows:

2020/21
April to September 2020 – Loss   £250,000

2019/20
October 2019 to March 2020 – Profit:
£85,000 x 6/12   (£42,500) profit – hence ignore

Hence, he has a 'terminal loss' of £250,000 and can claim to set this off against his previous three years' taxable income, with more recent years taken first, as follows:

2019/20: £85,000 – giving rise to a tax saving of £25,923
2018/19: £140,000 – giving rise to a tax repayment of £54,386
2017/18: £25,000* – giving rise to a tax repayment of £14,500

* The balance of the loss remaining after relieving the later years (£250,000 – £85,000 – £140,000 = £25,000)

By incorporating his business, Kim has been able to generate tax repayments and savings totalling £94,809, which is £68,886 more than he would have been able to achieve if he had simply continued in business as a sole trader.

Overlap Relief

As explained in Chapter 10, overlap relief is available when you cease trading, providing relief for overlap profits created when you started trading (see Chapter 10), or on a subsequent change of accounting date (see Chapter 12). Once again, incorporating your business is treated as ceasing to trade for this purpose.

Overlap relief may be included in a terminal loss relief claim and is not subject to the tax relief 'cap' (see Chapter 40), even when losses are being set off against other sources of income.

With many businesses seeing sharp falls in trading profits during the Coronavirus Crisis, now could be a good time to 'cash in' your overlap relief.

Example
Linda has overlap profits of £60,000 brought forward from her early years of trading. She has often considered changing her accounting date in order to obtain relief for these but would need to extend her accounting period by ten months to achieve this (see Chapter 12). Until February 2020 her monthly profits averaged over £10,000, so extending her accounting period was likely to lead to an increase in tax liabilities.

She made a profit of £110,000 for the year ending 30th April 2020 but then suffered losses of £1,000 per month until August 2020. She seizes her chance and incorporates her business on 1st September 2020.

If Linda had left things as they were, she would have had a taxable profit of £110,000 in 2020/21, giving rise to tax of £38,504. By incorporating she has reduced her taxable profit for 2020/21 as follows:

Profit for year ending 30th April 2020	*£110,000*
Losses for period May to August 2020	*(£4,000)*
Overlap relief	*(£60,000)*
Taxable profit	*£44,000*

This reduces her tax liability for 2020/21 to just £9,564, a saving of £28,940.

Chapter 33

Deferring Tax by Changing Company Accounting Dates

There is far less scope for saving tax by changing company accounting dates (compared with sole traders and partnerships – see Chapter 12).

Companies have been paying Corporation Tax at the same, single rate of 19% since 2017, and are currently expected to do so until at least March 2022. Hence any change of accounting date will not alter the amount of Corporation Tax paid in the long run; it will only alter the timing of tax payments.

As a general rule, there is normally a cashflow advantage for companies with seasonal businesses if they prepare accounts to a date shortly before their main profit season begins.

Hence, if you generally make most profits in the summer, a 30th April accounting date will ensure each summer's profits fall into the accounts ending on 30th April the following calendar year, meaning the relevant Corporation Tax payment is not due until 1st February the year after that – around eighteen months after the profits arose.

Similarly, if most of your sales arise in November or December, a 31st October accounting date will defer the Corporation Tax on your most profitable season until 1st August two calendar years later.

But things aren't really normal at the moment and a 31st March accounting date might mean the losses you make over the spring and summer of 2020 aren't providing you with any tax relief until 2022. That's too long to wait. Here's a better way to do it.

Example
Mila Ltd usually makes an annual profit of around £400,000. Profits for the year ended 31st March 2020 are slightly down, at £300,000, but the next six months are much worse, with management accounts showing a loss of £210,000. Conditions improve from October onwards

and projections for the full year show a probable final result for the year ending 31st March 2021 of around a £30,000 loss.

If Mila Ltd leaves things as they are, it will have a Corporation Tax bill of £57,000 (£300,000 x 19%) to pay on 1st January 2021 and might be able to claim a repayment of £5,700 (£30,000 x 19%) once its 2021 accounts are finalised and it has submitted its next Corporation Tax return. Mila herself (the company's owner) knows that's likely to take until at least June 2021, at best.

Instead, Mila changes the company's accounting date to 30th September by extending the company's accounting period from 31st March 2020 to 30th September 2020. The overall result for this eighteen month period is a profit of £90,000 (£300,000 - £210,000). The company now has to pay just £11,400 (£90,000 x 12/18 x 19%) on 1st January 2021, followed by a further £5,700 (£90,000 x 6/18 x 19%) on 1st July 2021.

By changing her company's accounting date, Mila has gained a cashflow advantage of £45,600 (£57,000 - £11,400) in January 2021 which will hugely aid the company's recovery. While this cashflow advantage will slightly diminish in July 2021 (to £39,900 – still a healthy saving), it will not fully reverse until July 2022, eighteen months after it was first generated.

The deadlines for changing company accounting dates are the same as for an LLP – see Chapter 12.

Chapter 34

Loss Relief

Despite the emergency measures and various forms of help provided by the Government (see Chapter 1), many businesses are likely to realise losses during accounting periods spanning, or including, the Coronavirus Crisis.

Tax relief is available for business losses in various forms, although these differ significantly depending on the type of business and the legal structure within which the business is carried out (sole trader, partnership, LLP, or company).

Many business owners will be interested in loss carry backs – relieving a current loss against earlier period's profits, income, etc, to provide immediate (or at least rapid) relief, or even a repayment. While this facility is available in some cases, it is not always possible to relieve losses in this way.

In previous periods of economic difficulty (such as the recession of the early 1990s, the foot and mouth crisis of 2001, and the banking crisis of 2008/9), the Government has been known to extend loss relief and my money would be on this happening again.

However, as yet, we only have the existing rules at our disposal. Over the next few chapters we will examine what they are.

Chapter 35

Company Losses

Loss relief for companies underwent a significant change in 2017 and is now more generous than before for small and medium-sized companies, although it is less generous for very large companies. So, what are the rules?

Company Trading Losses

In the first instance, trading losses may be set off against the company's other income and capital gains of the same accounting period.

Loss Carry Back

If the claim for set-off of trading losses within the same accounting period has been made, the company may additionally claim to carry back any surplus loss against its total profits and capital gains in the twelve months preceding the accounting period that gave rise to the loss.

If, however, the loss-making trade was not being carried on by the company throughout the previous twelve months, the relevant period for loss set-off is the period beginning with the commencement of that trade.

An added benefit of setting a trading loss off against other income in the current and previous years is that the resultant tax saving is more or less immediate.

Loss Carry Forward

Any trading losses that still remain unrelieved after any claim for set-off in the current year or carry back to the previous year, will be carried forward for set-off as follows:

- Losses arising after 31st March 2017 may be set off against the company's total income and capital gains, provided the trade that gave rise to the loss has not ceased or become 'small'. Where the trade has become 'small', the carried forward losses may only be set off against future profits from that trade. Here there is no definition of what 'small' means, although it seems safe to assume it means the trade has become far smaller than it was when it gave rise to the losses.

- Losses arising before 1st April 2017 may only be set off against future profits from the same trade.

Companies must now claim these set-offs and are subject to limits on amounts in excess of £5m, as discussed below.

Group Relief

Companies that are members of a group of companies may also surrender some or all of their trading losses as group relief.

Claim Deadlines

Loss relief claims must be made within two years of the end of the loss-making accounting period in the case of losses set off against profits and capital gains within the same period or the previous twelve months; or within two years of the end of the period for which relief is claimed in the case of losses carried forward.

Company Rental Losses

Before we discuss rental losses arising in a company, it is important to understand that interest and finance costs incurred in connection with a company's property investment or property letting business are treated as general overheads of the company rather than expenses of the letting business (except in the case of furnished holiday lets – see below).

Example
In the year ending 31st December 2020, Emilia Ltd has rental income of £60,000, sundry allowable expenses of £25,000 and interest and finance costs of £50,000.

From an internal accounting perspective, the company is reporting a rental loss of £15,000, as you would expect. However, for tax purposes, the company is treated as having a rental profit of £35,000 (£60,000 – £25,000).

All is not lost as Emilia Ltd can, of course, set £35,000 of its interest costs against its taxable rental profit, leaving it with no Corporation Tax to pay. Phew!

This leaves £15,000 of its interest cost unrelieved, and this sum will be available for relief as discussed below, under 'Surplus Interest Costs'.

Given the fact that interest and finance costs incurred in connection with a company's property rental business are not generally treated as an expense of that business, rental losses within a company should be a fairly rare occurrence. Nonetheless, let's look at what happens when such losses do arise.

For loss relief purposes, we must divide the company's property lettings into four categories:
i)   Ordinary UK property lettings
ii)   Ordinary overseas lettings
iii)   UK furnished holiday lets
iv)   Furnished holiday lets in the European Economic Area

For the purposes of (i) and (ii) above, 'ordinary' simply means not a furnished holiday let.

Ordinary UK Property Lettings

Subject to the exception for non-commercial lettings set out below, for Corporation Tax purposes, all of a company's 'ordinary' UK property lettings are treated as a single UK property business. Hence, the loss on any one such property is automatically set off against profits on other commercially let UK properties for the same period.

Any overall net losses arising from a company's 'ordinary' UK property-letting business will be set off against the company's other income and capital gains for the same period (if any). This represents a major advantage over individual property investors, or partnerships: who can only carry forward any net rental loss (other than losses derived from capital allowances) – see Chapter 37.

Any remaining surplus rental loss incurred by the company is carried forward and set off against the company's total profits (including capital gains) for the next accounting period, then the next, and so on. Rental losses may be carried forward for as long as is necessary in this way, provided the company is still carrying on an 'ordinary' UK property-letting business in the accounting period for which the claim to offset the losses is made.

If the company's 'ordinary' UK property-letting business ceases, but the company still has an 'investment business', then any unused UK rental losses are converted to 'management expenses'. 'Management expenses' may also be carried forward and set off against the company's total profits, including capital gains, for as long as the company continues to have an 'investment business'.

An 'investment business' is any business that consists of making investments. For example, the company may have an 'investment business' if:

- It owns subsidiary companies
- It has foreign investment property
- It holds a portfolio of stock market investments

It is questionable, however, whether simply holding cash on deposit constitutes an 'investment business'.

It is unclear whether furnished holiday lets constitute an 'investment business' for these purposes; so it would perhaps be unwise to rely on them as a means to preserve rental losses from an 'ordinary' UK property-letting business.

Nevertheless, it is clear there are many ways for a company to preserve the value of its 'ordinary' UK rental losses and ensure Corporation Tax relief is ultimately obtained. This contrasts with individual investors, who effectively lose the value of 'ordinary' UK rental losses if they cease to carry on an 'ordinary' UK rental business (see Chapter 37).

A company will only lose the value of its unused rental losses if it ceases to carry on both its 'ordinary' UK letting business and any other type of 'investment business'.

Ordinary Overseas Lettings

All of a company's 'ordinary' overseas lettings are treated as a single business for Corporation Tax purposes. This is treated as a separate business to the company's UK property letting business (if any).

Any loss on this business may be carried forward and set off against future profits from the same business – i.e. against future 'ordinary' overseas rental profits received by the company.

Furnished Holiday Lets

All of a company's UK furnished holiday lets are treated as a single business. All of its furnished holiday lets in the European Economic Area are also treated as a single business – but a different one.

Losses arising on a furnished holiday letting business may only be carried forward and set off against future profits from the same business.

Here, losses are far more likely to arise (even under normal circumstances) as interest and finance costs relating to a furnished holiday letting business are treated as deductible costs of that business and not as general company overheads. Hence, the inability to set losses against other types of income, or capital gains, is severely restrictive, especially during the Coronavirus Crisis.

We will return to look more closely at this badly-stricken sector in Chapter 39, which also includes a definition of furnished holiday lets.

Non-Commercial Lettings

Losses arising on any non-commercial lettings (i.e. lettings not made on normal, commercial, 'arm's length' terms) may only be set against future profits from the same letting. This includes interest and finance costs incurred in connection with any such lettings

Surplus Interest Costs

Interest and finance costs incurred in connection with the company's property investment, or property letting, business may be set off against any income or capital gains received by the company during the same accounting period.

Furthermore, as an alternative, the company may instead:

i)   Carry the costs back for set off against any interest, and certain other limited categories of income, received in the previous year,

ii)   Carry the costs forward for set off against any income or capital gains in future periods, or

iii)   Surrender the costs as 'group relief' (where the company is a member of a group of companies)

For costs arising before April 2017, any amounts carried forward under (ii) can only be set off against non-trading income or capital gains in future periods. Since this includes rental profits, it will seldom cause an issue for property investment companies.

The carry forward rules under (ii) are subject to the proviso that the company must continue to carry on an investment business. An investment business for this purpose includes any form of property letting other than furnished holiday lets, as well as the other categories of investment business referred to above, although the investment business must not be 'small'. Again, there is no definition of what 'small' means, although it seems safe to assume it means very small indeed.

If the company ceases to have an investment business, or it becomes 'small' then amounts carried forward under (ii) will again only be eligible for set off against non-trading income and capital gains. Note that furnished holiday letting profits (see Chapter 39) are classed as trading income for the purposes of (ii) and are thus ineligible for the set off of brought forward interest and finance costs arising before April 2017 (or later costs when the company's investment business has ceased or become 'small').

Restrictions on interest relief apply to large companies that are members of international groups. Companies with no more than £2m of annual interest costs, or with no overseas associated companies, are not affected, however.

Corporate Loss Relief Restrictions

The total amount of relief which a company, or group of companies, may claim for brought forward losses and unrelieved interest and finance costs is restricted to a maximum of £5m plus 50% of any profits in excess of that amount. The £5m limit applies on an annual basis (e.g. the limit would be £2.5m for a six month period).

Chapter 36

Trading Losses

This chapter covers trading losses realised by unincorporated businesses. For the treatment of trading losses in companies, see Chapter 35.

Various forms of relief are available for trading losses realised by unincorporated businesses. We will start with the main reliefs available at any time and then move on to additional reliefs available at the beginning and end of a trading business's life.

Note that loss relief for unincorporated business owners is subject to the tax relief 'cap' explained in Chapter 40.

It is also critical to note that the loss relief provisions described below are not available on losses arising under the 'cash basis' (see Chapter 31). Such losses may only be carried forward for set off against future profits from the same trade.

The Main Reliefs

The general rule is you may claim to set trading losses off against your total income for the same tax year and/or the previous one. Where you have claimed to set your losses off against income in one of these years (or you have no such income), you may also claim to set any further losses remaining against capital gains arising in the same year. This gives rise to a number of possible choices (I count eight!)

Any surplus loss remaining is automatically carried forward for set off against future profits from the same trade. This effectively gives rise to a ninth choice: make no claim under the above provisions and carry all your losses forward.

National Insurance and Losses

Note that losses set against trading profits will provide relief for both Income Tax and Class 4 National Insurance purposes.

However, where trading losses are set against employment income in the same or previous tax year, there is no relief for Class 1 National Insurance purposes.

Early Years

Under a separate provision, losses arising in any of the first four tax years of a new trade may also be carried back against your total income in the three tax years prior to the loss-making year. The loss is relieved against earlier years first.

Example
Felicity worked in a bank for many years. She was quite high up, earning a salary of £125,000 in 2017/18. She earned a further £33,000 between April and June 2018 but then she quit: she'd had enough. In September 2018, she set up a florist business, 'Feliciflora'. Her trading results were as follows:

Period ended 31st March 2019: Profit of £10,000
Year ended 31st March 2020: Profit of £50,000
*Year ended 31st March 2021: **Loss** of £25,000*

If Felicity carried her loss back to 2019/20 under the main provisions set out above (which are still available to her), she would save just £7,250 in Income Tax and National Insurance (at 29% - see Chapter 13).

Instead, however, under the 'early years' loss relief provisions, she can carry her 2020/21 loss back to 2017/18 and obtain a repayment of the Income Tax suffered on the top £25,000 of her salary, as follows:

£25,000 @ 40% = £10,000
£11,500 @ 40% = £4,600 (she recovers her 2017/18 personal allowance, originally withdrawn from her)
*Total repayment: **£14,600***

Now, that ought to help get Felicity started again!

Terminal Losses

Under yet another provision, known as 'terminal loss relief', losses arising in the last twelve months of a trade (including 'overlap relief' – see Chapters 10 and 12) may be carried back against income in the final tax year of the trade and the previous three tax years. In this case, the loss is relieved against the most recent years first.

This includes cases where the trade is incorporated (i.e. transferred to a company). We will look at the potential benefits of this in Chapter 32, which also provides a good example of how terminal loss relief operates in practice.

Exercising Your Options

As we can see, there are many possible ways to relieve trading losses, especially in the early years of a new business. The best choice will depend on the effective tax rates applying in each year and the likelihood of you making profits from the same trade in the future. You generally have until one year after the 31st January following the tax year to decide (the deadline for making claims under most of the above provisions). For example, a claim in respect of a loss arising during 2020/21 must generally be made by 31st January 2023.

Whatever choice you make, it is important to remember the same loss can only ever be relieved once. However, where more than one choice is available to you then, subject to the rules described above, you are able to decide which claim to make first, with the remaining loss then available for other claims. For example, you could make a claim to set losses off against your other income in the same tax year first and then make an 'early years' loss relief claim (where applicable) in respect of your remaining losses.

For the purposes of trading loss relief, partners are treated as commencing a trade when they join a trading partnership and as ceasing to trade when they leave the partnership.

The same applies to members of an LLP. However, LLP members carrying on a trading business (but not, in this case, a profession), are not entitled to 'early years loss relief' (so it's a good job Felicity didn't set up an LLP).

Sole traders or partnerships transferring a trade to a company (often known as 'incorporation') are treated as ceasing to trade on the date of the transfer. Note, however, that losses which cannot be relieved under any of the above provisions will effectively be lost: they cannot be transferred to the company. For more details of the potential benefits of incorporation, see Chapter 32.

Loss Relief Restrictions

As discussed above, where trading losses are being set off against income (not capital gains), the relief is subject to the tax relief 'cap' explained in Chapter 40. This does not apply where the losses are being set against profits from the same trade, or to the extent that the losses include 'overlap relief' (see Chapters 10 and 12).

In addition, a 'non-active sole trader' may only claim tax relief against his or her other income and gains for a maximum of just £25,000 of trading losses each year. Personally, I find the term 'non-active sole trader' to be as much of a contradiction in terms as an 'honest politician', but it is taken to mean someone who spends less than ten hours per week engaged in trading activities. Sadly, this restriction may hit many part-time traders. For those whose business activities average only just over the ten hours per week threshold, it will make sense to keep diaries or other time records to demonstrate hours spent.

Loss relief is also barred for trading losses of a 'non-active sole trader' arising as a result of arrangements made for tax avoidance purposes.

Similar restrictions apply to 'non-active partners', which have much the same definition.

Chapter 37

Rental Losses

This chapter covers rental losses realised by unincorporated businesses. For the treatment of rental losses, or surplus interest costs, in companies, see Chapter 35.

Losses on furnished holiday lets are also subject to different rules, which we will look at in Chapter 39.

Note that, due to the dreadful restriction on interest relief imposed by the Government (see Chapter 21), surplus interest and finance costs relating to residential lettings are no longer treated as rental losses but are now regarded as 'excess interest costs'. We will look at the treatment of these in Chapter 38.

First, however, let's look at the rules on rental losses.

Rental Losses on UK Property

All your UK property lettings, apart from furnished holiday lets (see Chapter 39), are treated as a single UK property business. For loss relief purposes, however, it is necessary to separate UK rental property into three categories:

- Non-commercial lettings
- Furnished holiday lettings
- Other UK rental property (which I will refer to as 'normal' rental property for the sake of illustration)

Losses arising on furnished holiday lettings or non-commercial lettings are subject to special rules, which we will look at in Chapter 39 and later in this chapter, respectively.

Losses arising on 'normal' rental property are automatically set off against profits on other 'normal' UK rental property for the same period. Losses on 'normal' UK rental property may also be set off against profits on non-commercial lettings. Any overall net losses from 'normal' rental property remaining after this may be carried forward and set off against future profits from 'normal' UK rental property or non-commercial lettings.

Losses consisting of capital allowances may also be set off against the landlord's other income of the same tax year or the next one (subject to the tax relief 'cap' discussed in Chapter 40).

Example
In the tax year 2020/21, Gates has employment income of £70,000, from which he suffers deduction of tax under PAYE totalling £15,500. He also has a portfolio of rented commercial property on which he has made an overall loss of £15,000, including £10,000 of capital allowances. Gates can claim to set his capital allowances off against his employment income, which will produce a tax repayment of £4,000.

How Long Can Rental Losses Be Carried Forward?

Rental losses from 'normal' rental property may be carried forward for as long as you continue to have a 'normal' UK property rental business. There are two major pitfalls to watch out for here.

Firstly, rental losses are personal. They cannot be transferred to another person, not even your spouse, and they do not transfer with the properties. If you die with rental losses, they die with you.

Secondly, if your 'normal' UK property business ceases, you will lose your losses. It may therefore be vital to keep your 'normal' UK property business going. As long as you continue to have at least one 'normal' UK rental property, you still have a 'normal' UK property business.

HMRC will sometimes accept that a total cessation of all 'normal' rental income is not necessarily the same as a cessation of your 'normal' UK rental business, especially where the rental properties are still held. They will usually accept that the rental business has not ceased:

- Where you can provide evidence that you have been attempting unsuccessfully to let out your property, or
- Where rental has only ceased temporarily whilst repairs or alterations are carried out

These points may be especially important for landlords with empty properties during the Coronavirus Crisis.

HMRC will, however, generally regard the rental business as having ceased if there is a gap of more than three years between lettings and different properties are let before and after the gap. They may sometimes accept a gap of less than three years as not being a cessation, but not if you have clearly employed all your capital in some other type of business, or spent it for personal purposes, such as buying yourself a new home.

Losses on Overseas Lettings

All of a taxpayer's commercially let overseas properties (with the exception of any furnished holiday lets within the European Economic Area, 'EEA') are treated as a single business in much the same way as, but separate from, a UK property business.

Furnished holiday lets within the EEA are subject to the same special regime as qualifying furnished holiday lets in the UK, although, again, these are treated as a separate business. See Chapter 39 for further details.

The UK tax treatment of losses arising from an overseas letting business is exactly the same as for a UK property business except, of course, that this is treated as a separate business from any UK lettings the taxpayer has. Hence, again, for loss relief purposes, overseas property must be separated into three categories, as follows:

- Non-commercial overseas lettings (see below)
- Furnished holiday lettings within the EEA
- Other overseas rental property (which I will refer to as 'normal' overseas property for the sake of illustration)

Losses arising on 'normal' overseas property are automatically set off against profits derived from other 'normal' overseas lettings or non-commercial overseas lettings, with the excess carried forward for set off against future 'normal' overseas rental profits. The same rule as set out above for 'normal' UK property applies to any capital allowances.

Where there are substantial 'normal' overseas rental losses carried forward, it will be worthwhile ensuring this business continues. The same principles as set out above for 'normal' UK property apply here, except that, to continue the business, it is necessary to continue to have 'normal' overseas rental property. While the property must be let on a commercial basis, and must be outside the UK, it can be in any other part of the world and need not be in the same country as the property that gave rise to the original losses. A loss made in Albania might conceivably be set off against a profit in Zanzibar!

As before, however, it is essential to remember that a qualifying furnished holiday letting property within the EEA will not suffice to preserve rental losses from 'normal' overseas property.

Non-Commercial Lettings

Where lettings are not on a commercial or 'arm's length' basis, they cannot be regarded as part of the same UK or overseas property business as any commercial lettings the taxpayer has. Profits remain taxable, but any losses arising may only be carried forward for set off against future profits from the same letting (i.e. the same property let to the same tenant).

Typically, this type of letting involves the lease of a property to a relative or friend at a nominal rent, considerably less than the full market rent the property could demand on the open market.

Chapter 38

Excess Interest for Residential Landlords

As explained in Chapter 21, from 2020/21, interest and finance costs on residential lettings are no longer properly deductible from rental income (as they really ought to be Mr Osborne!) but are only eligible for basic rate tax relief at 20%.

In 2019/20, 25% of the relevant costs were properly deductible, with the remaining 75% only eligible for basic rate tax relief. (The 25% element still allowed as a proper deduction in 2019/20 remains subject to the old rules, and may form part of a rental loss, to be dealt with as set out in Chapter 37.)

These abominable provisions do not apply to companies (see Chapter 35), furnished holiday lets (see Chapter 39), or commercial (non-residential) property letting. Excess interest on non-residential lettings forms part of the landlord's rental losses and is dealt with as set out in Chapter 37.

In addition, the treatment of any surplus, or 'excess', interest and finance costs on residential lettings has changed. Excess interest and finance costs on residential lettings is carried forward and may only be set off against future taxable rental profits from residential lettings, with relief, once again, restricted to basic rate. As usual, UK and overseas property businesses must be kept separate.

Example
Izabella has an annual salary of £50,000, as well as a large residential rental property portfolio. In 2020/21, due to a number of voids and bad debts (see Chapter 16), she has rental profits before interest of just £20,000 and interest costs of £30,000. This means she has excess interest and finance costs of £10,000 (they cannot be set against her employment income) to be carried forward.

In 2021/22, things improve for Izabella and she has rental profits before interest of £60,000. She is now able to claim basic rate relief for the excess interest costs of £10,000, as well as the £30,000 of interest costs incurred in 2021/22.

How Much Interest Attracts Basic Rate Tax Relief?

The amount of interest and finance costs on residential property that attracts basic rate tax relief is the lowest of the following three amounts:

i)   The total qualifying interest and finance costs on residential property for the year less (for years up to 2019/20) the proportion allowed as a direct deduction against rental profits, PLUS any unrelieved excess interest brought forward

ii)   The taxable residential rental profits for the year

iii)   The landlord's total taxable income for the year, excluding interest income, other savings income, and dividends; and after deducting their personal allowance

The unrelieved interest brought forward under (i) means excess interest and finance costs on residential lettings arising in tax years from 2017/18 onwards that can only be relieved at basic rate – see the Taxcafe.co.uk guide *How to Save Property Tax* for further details. This amount does not include interest that is fully deductible and is included within rental losses brought forward.

For landlords with profitable (before tax) residential property letting businesses who also have:

a)   Total true rental profits (after deducting interest and finance costs), including profits from furnished holiday lets and non-residential lettings,

b)   Earned income,

c)   Pension income, or

d)   Any combination of the above

In excess of the personal allowance, the restrictions set out above are unlikely to have any practical effect and these landlords should be able to claim basic rate tax relief on all their interest and finance costs.

In other words, in these cases, the amount under (i) above (total qualifying interest and finance costs less, in years up to 2019/20, the proportion allowed as a direct deduction) will usually be the lowest amount and will thus be the amount on which they claim basic rate tax relief.

Consequently, most landlords with profitable (before tax) residential property letting businesses will not have and excess interest to carry forward.

However, the position may differ for some landlords with little or no other income.

Example

In both 2019/20 and 2020/21, Halle has residential rental profits of £30,000 before deduction of interest and finance costs totalling £24,000. She has no other income.

In 2019/20, 25% of Halle's interest costs, or £6,000, is deducted directly from her rental income, leaving her with £24,000 of taxable income. This exceeds the 2019/20 personal allowance of £12,500 by £11,500.

Halle has a further £18,000 of interest and finance costs eligible for relief at basic rate (75% of her total cost for the year). However, the amount eligible for relief is restricted to £11,500: the amount by which her taxable income exceeds the personal allowance.

Halle therefore has no tax to pay for 2019/20 and unrelieved excess interest and finance costs of £6,500 to carry forward.

In 2020/21, she is unable to deduct any of her interest costs directly against her rental income, meaning she has £30,000 of taxable income, which exceeds the 2020/21 personal allowance of £12,500 by £17,500. She is therefore able to claim basic rate relief on £17,500 of her interest cost, leaving her with no tax to pay for 2020/21 and a further £6,500 (£24,000 - £17,500) of unrelieved excess interest and finance costs to carry forward.

She now has a total of £13,000 (£6,500 + £6,500) of excess interest carried forward which could save her £2,600 in a later year when her rental profits are higher, or she has taxable income from other sources.

This example illustrates the only bit of good news about the Government's diabolical interest relief restrictions: landlords like Halle, whose overall income is quite low, are able to carry forward some of their interest and finance costs rather than set them against income that is covered by their personal allowance.

In other words, such landlords will get effective tax relief for their interest and finance costs (albeit in the future and restricted to basic rate) rather than wasting them as a deduction against income that would not have been taxed anyway.

Order of Relief

Where a landlord has both rental losses and excess interest costs brought forward, the rental losses are set off first, in priority to the excess interest. Over time, this will often have the effect of converting fully relievable rental losses into excess interest relievable at basic rate only. See the Taxcafe.co.uk guide *How to Save Property Tax* for further details.

Chapter 39

Furnished Holiday Lets

This is one of the sectors that will suffer the greatest hardships during the Coronavirus Crisis and yet, as things stand, as far as loss relief is concerned, there is very little scope to claim any relief.

Losses arising in a furnished holiday letting business may only be carried forward for set off against future profits from the same furnished holiday letting business. For this purpose, all of a landlord's UK furnished holiday lets are regarded as one business but furnished holiday lets elsewhere in the EEA (see below) are regarded as a different business. (All furnished holiday lets within the EEA but outside the UK are regarded as the same business)

Interest and finance costs relating to a furnished holiday letting business are fully deductible costs and will form part of furnished holiday letting losses, where appropriate.

Despite the restrictions on loss relief, furnished holiday letting status is normally quite attractive, since:

- Capital allowances are available
- The restrictions on interest relief applying to residential lettings do not apply to furnished holiday lets
- furnished holiday lets are eligible for a number of Capital Gains Tax reliefs, including entrepreneurs' relief, holdover relief, incorporation relief and rollover relief

Qualifying Conditions
To qualify as a furnished holiday let, the property must meet the qualifying conditions for the relevant period. The relevant period is normally the tax year for individuals, or the accounting period for companies. However, when the property begins or ceases to be let out fully furnished, then it is the first or last twelve months for which it is so let (see below for the definition of 'fully furnished').

The qualifying conditions are that the property must be:

i)   Situated in the UK or the European Economic Area (see below)
ii)   Fully furnished (see below)
iii) Let out on a commercial basis with a view to the realisation of profits
iv)   Available for letting as holiday accommodation to the public generally for at least 210 days
v)   Actually let as holiday accommodation to members of the public for at least 105 days
vi)   Not in 'longer term occupation' for more than 155 days

'Longer term occupation' means any period of more than 31 consecutive days during which the property is in the same occupation, unless this arises due to exceptional circumstances (e.g. the tenant falls ill, or their flight home is delayed). Periods of longer term occupation cannot be counted towards the 105 days required under condition (v).

A taxpayer with more than one furnished holiday let may use a system of averaging to determine whether they meet condition (v).

Landlords can elect for properties that qualified in the previous year (including those qualifying by using averaging, as above) to stay within the regime for up to two further tax years, despite failing to meet condition (v). In effect, this means properties generally only need to meet this test once every three years. The property must meet the other qualifying conditions and the landlord must have had a genuine intention to meet condition (v) each year.

This last rule is going to be particularly critical during 2020/21, when many landlords will struggle to let out their properties for the requisite 105 days, due to the Coronavirus Crisis. We may see some special relaxation of the rules to deal with this situation but, in the meantime, it remains important to meet the other tests in 2020/21 if you want your property to maintain its furnished holiday let status.

What is the European Economic Area ('EEA')?

The EEA comprises the 27 member states of the European Union, plus Iceland, Liechtenstein and Norway.

What Is a Fully Furnished Letting?

To be classed as a 'fully furnished letting', the landlord must provide sufficient furnishings so the property is capable of 'normal residential use' without the tenant having to provide their own. Typically, this will include beds, chairs, tables, sofas, carpets or other floor coverings, curtains or blinds, and kitchen equipment.

The key phrase here is whether the property is capable of 'normal residential use' and the level of furnishings and equipment required must be considered in this context. In essence, the landlord must provide the tenant with some privacy, somewhere to sit, somewhere to sleep, somewhere to eat, and the facilities required to feed themselves.

Chapter 40

The Tax Relief 'Cap'

There is an annual limit on the total combined amount of Income Tax relief available under a number of different reliefs. The total amount that any individual may claim under all these reliefs taken together in any tax year is limited to the greater of £50,000 or 25% of their 'adjusted total income' (see below).

The Affected Reliefs

Ten different reliefs are affected. The most important ones for unincorporated business owners to be aware of are:

- Relief for trading losses against other income
- Property loss relief
- Qualifying loan interest
- Share loss relief

Relief for trading losses is covered in Chapter 36.

'Property loss relief' refers to your ability to set capital allowances within UK rental losses or overseas rental losses against your other income for the same tax year or the next one (see Chapter 37).

'Qualifying loan interest' is the relief which is given for interest on personal borrowings used to invest funds in a qualifying company (or partnership). This relief will often be claimed by property investors who invest via a company and is covered in detail in the Taxcafe.co.uk guide 'Using a Property Company to Save Tax'.

'Share loss relief' applies in limited circumstances and allows owners of some private companies to claim Income Tax relief for share losses. Not usually available for property company shares.

Adjusted Total Income

Broadly speaking, 'adjusted total income' means an individual's total taxable income for the year in which relief is being claimed; after deducting gross pension contributions (including tax relief given at source); but before deducting any other reliefs.

Chapter 41

Is This a Good Time to Transfer Property?

With property values likely to fall during the Coronavirus Crisis, this may be a good time to make property transfers. The benefits of transferring property into your own company while values are depressed are examined in Chapter 32. Other transfers you may wish to consider at this time are transfers to your children, or other heirs, an unmarried partner, or into a trust. Most of these transfers tend to be made for Inheritance Tax planning purposes, although there are other reasons too.

Stamp Duty Land Tax (or equivalent)

Transfers made by way of gift do not usually attract Stamp Duty Land Tax (or its equivalents in Scotland and Wales), unless the transferee takes on a share of the mortgage or other debt, and their share of the debt amounts to £40,000 or more (see the Taxcafe.co.uk guide *How to Save Property Tax* for further details).

Hence, with the exception of transfers into your own company (see Chapter 32), Stamp Duty Land Tax will be unaffected by any fall in property values.

Capital Gains Tax Savings

Transfers to a spouse are free from Capital Gains Tax (providing you hadn't separated before the beginning of the tax year) and can therefore generally be carried out free from tax at any time (but see the Taxcafe.co.uk guide *How to Save Property Tax* regarding Stamp Duty Land Tax and its equivalents where there is a mortgage on the property).

The gain arising on a gift of furnished holiday lets or property used in your own trading business can be 'held over' so that no Capital Gains Tax is due. In essence, the taxable gain is effectively deferred until the transferee ultimately disposes of the property themselves.

However, transfers of other types of property to individuals other than your spouse (e.g. to your children) will generally mean you have to pay Capital Gains Tax as if you had sold the property at its market value at the date of transfer. For UK residential property disposals taking place after 5th April 2020, any taxable capital gain arising must be reported within 30 days and a reasonable estimate of the Capital Gains Tax due paid by the same date.

Hence, it is these other types of property where a reduction in market value during the Coronavirus Crisis may give you the opportunity to make a transfer with a more acceptable Capital Gains Tax cost than previously.

Example 1.1

Naoko is a higher rate taxpayer and owns a portfolio of residential rental properties. She is looking to pass some of her properties on to her son in order to reduce the Inheritance Tax arising on her death. She has considered the trust route (see below) but, as the total value of her properties is well in excess of £325,000, this alone will not resolve the problem.

Two of her properties were bought in 2007 for £80,000 each and, even before Coronavirus Crisis had only shown modest increases in value to around £110,000 each. Naoko had been considering transferring one property to her son in 2020/21 and one in 2021/22 and had calculated that the Capital Gains Tax arising on each transfer would have been £4,956, a total of £9,912.

However, by June 2020, the properties have fallen in value to £88,000 each. Naoko seizes her chance and transfers both properties while their values are depressed. Each property realises a gain of just £8,000, giving her total gains for the tax year of £16,000. After deducting her annual Capital Gains Tax exemption of £12,300, her taxable gain is just £3,700, giving rise to a Capital Gains Tax bill, at 28%, of a mere £1,036.

Not only has Naoko saved £8,876, she's managed to transfer two properties straight away instead of having to wait until 2021/22 to make the second transfer.

Additional Capital Gains Tax Savings Where Taxable Income Reduced

If the transferor's taxable income for the tax year is reduced below the higher-rate tax threshold (currently £50,000) due to the Coronavirus Crisis, there may be a further Capital Gains Tax saving on property transfers taking place this year.

For example, in Naoko's case, if her taxable income for 2020/21 is reduced below £50,000 and she becomes a basic rate taxpayer this year, the Capital Gains Tax rate on some or all of her taxable gain would fall from 28% to 18%, saving her up to a further £370 in Capital Gains Tax.

In some cases, where the taxpayer's total taxable income for the year is reduced below the personal allowance (£12,500), the additional Capital Gains Tax saving on property transfers made this year (2020/21) could be as much as £3,750. This saving is created by the 10% differential between the Capital Gains Tax rates on gains accruing to higher rate taxpayers and the rates on gains falling within the basic rate band (£37,500 for 2020/21).

The same 10% differential applies to most capital gains (with the exception of gains eligible for entrepreneurs' relief). Although the basic rate band is used up by income first, where any of it remains available to cover capital gains, the Capital Gains Tax rate on any gains falling within the basic rate band reduces:

- From 28% to 18% for gains on disposals of residential property (and 'carried interest', whatever that is)
- From 20% to 10% for gains on disposals of non-residential property, company shares, and any other assets

Inheritance Tax Savings

A lifetime gift to another individual is a 'Potentially Exempt Transfer' for Inheritance Tax purposes. What this means is that the transfer becomes fully exempt from Inheritance Tax after seven years.

However, if the transferor dies within seven years of making the gift, the value of that gift is effectively clawed back into their estate for Inheritance Tax purposes. BUT, here's the key point: it's the value at the time of the gift that is clawed back.

Hence, in Naoko's case (per our example above), if she were to die within seven years, the value to be 'clawed back' will now be only £176,000 (2 x £88,000) instead of £220,000 (2 x £110,000), a reduction of £44,000, saving her family up to £17,600 (£44,000 x 40%) in Inheritance Tax.

These potential Inheritance Tax savings also continue to apply to the vast majority of furnished holiday lets since, although these can usually be transferred free of Capital Gains Tax they will usually still be subject to Inheritance Tax.

Transfers into Trust

Capital Gains Tax can be avoided on a transfer of property into trust by making a hold over relief claim. In this case, the relief is available for any type of property.

However, the reason the Capital Gains Tax relief is so generous is that lifetime transfers into trust are chargeable lifetime transfers for Inheritance Tax purposes. If you make chargeable lifetime transfers in excess of the nil rate band (currently £325,000) within any seven year period, the excess will immediately be subject to Inheritance Tax at the lifetime rate of 20%. Further Inheritance Tax may also arise if you die within seven years of making the transfer.

Here, again, a fall in property values may make this easier.

Example 1.2
After gifting the two properties to her son in Example 1.1, Naoko is left with a further eight residential rental properties which were worth £200,000 each before the Coronavirus Crisis. She was previously advised that to even transfer two of these into trust would give rise to an immediate Inheritance Tax charge of £15,000, which would be increased to £18,750 in the highly probable event that she settled the tax herself. Furthermore, a subsequent transfer of the properties to her son in a future year might cost further tax, although it was nonetheless advisable to do this within ten years.

In July 2020, however, she has her properties revalued and discovers they are now worth only £162,000 each. She is now able to transfer two properties into trust without giving rise to any Inheritance Tax charge. Furthermore, there will be no charge on a subsequent transfer of the properties to her son taking place within the next ten years.

For the sake of illustration, I have assumed Naoko has already utilised her annual exemption for Inheritance Tax purposes of £3,000.

Chargeable lifetime transfers are also effectively clawed back into the estate if the transferor dies within seven years, although any tax paid on the original transfer may be deducted from the Inheritance Tax arising. Hence, the reduced values applying to Naoko's transfers into trust could save her family up to a further £30,400 in Inheritance Tax (£200,000 - £162,000 = £38,000 reduction in value per property; which is £76,000 in total, which saves Inheritance Tax at 40%).

Using trusts, or even making direct gifts to your children or other heirs, to save Inheritance Tax, is a complex subject, with many factors to consider. For further information see the Taxcafe.co.uk guide *'How to Save Inheritance Tax'*.

Chapter 42

Crystallising Losses

In Chapter 41, we looked at the benefits of realising smaller capital gains while values are reduced during the Coronavirus Crisis. What about crystallising capital losses?

The first thing to be wary of is that a capital loss arising on a transfer to a 'connected person' (typically a close relative such as a child, parent, or sibling) or on another transfer not made on 'arm's length terms' (typically to an unmarried partner, close friend, or a relative not defined as a 'connected person') cannot be set off against capital gains generally and can only be set off against a capital gain arising on another transfer to the same person. (So, if Naoko in Example 1.1 in Chapter 41 transferred two properties to her son, one at a gain and one at a loss, the loss could be set off against the gain on the other transfer, but not against any other gains she has.)

So, to crystallise a capital loss that is available to set against capital gains generally, you will generally need to actually sell assets at a loss. That, of course, means you are taking a real commercial loss on the asset: something most people are generally reluctant to do.

However, if you wish (or need) to sell the asset and you do realise a capital loss, this is automatically set off against any gains you make in the same tax year (including gains you make on transfers to 'connected persons' etc).

Any surplus net capital loss for the tax year is carried forward and set off against capital gains in future years, but only to the extent necessary to reduce them down to the annual exemption. This means timing your losses and gains carefully can provide Capital Gains Tax savings.

Example
Olga is a higher rate taxpayer with three residential investment properties that she wishes to sell: Quanta House; Offa House; and Sola House.

Olga sells Quanta House in October 2020 and realises a capital loss of £28,000. In March 2021, she is ready to sell Offa House and will realise a capital gain of £30,000. If she sells Offa House by 5ᵗʰ April 2021, her capital loss will automatically be set off against her capital gain, leaving her with a net capital gain of just £2,000. This will be covered by her annual exemption, leaving her with no Capital Gains Tax to pay, but it will mean her capital losses from Quanta House have been fully utilised.

However, if she defers her sale of Offa House until at least 6ᵗʰ April 2021, so that it falls into the 2021/22 tax year, the first £12,300 of her gain will be covered by her annual exemption (see Appendix), and only £17,700 of her capital loss will be used against the remainder, leaving £10,300 to be carried forward.

If she then sells Sola House in 2022/23, she will have a capital loss of £10,300 still available to reduce her Capital Gains Tax bill by £2,884 (£10,300 x 28%).

Note that the date of sale of a property (or any asset) for Capital Gains Tax purposes, is the date of unconditional contract. For residential property sales in England or Wales, this will generally be the date contracts are exchanged. In Scotland it is usually the date missives are concluded.

Lastly, please note that **capital losses cannot be carried back** for relief in an earlier tax year. Hence, crystallising losses during 2020/21 will be of no help in reducing your Capital Gains Tax bill for 2019/20.

Chapter 43

Avoiding Tax on Gifts

Many people are making, or considering, cash gifts to their children, or other relatives, to help them through this difficult time.

A direct gift to another individual is a 'Potentially Exempt Transfer' for Inheritance Tax purposes. This means that, as long as you survive at least seven years after making the gift, it will be exempt from Inheritance Tax.

However, HMRC have been known to attempt to reclassify gifts as mere loans, thus bringing them back into the deceased's estate for Inheritance Tax purposes and making them subject to Inheritance Tax, even if made more than seven years previously (I have absolutely no idea how these people sleep at night).

Hence, it is important to have a written record confirming that the sum you have given is indeed a gift. This is also an opportunity to specify who will bear any Inheritance Tax arising if you should unfortunately die within seven years. Normally, if you do not specify this, the liability (if any) will fall on the recipient of the gift and you may not want that – although sometimes, you will. It's up to you.

Here are a couple of suitable sample documents to use anyway:

Memorandum recording a gift where the transferor wishes to bear any Inheritance Tax arising

MEMORANDUM OF GIFT FROM
Patsy Hill of 6 Slade Street, Wolverhampton

TO
Raquel Holder of 9 Flame Avenue, Birmingham

MEMORANDUM that on 10th April 2020 Patsy Hill transferred by way of gift to Raquel Holder the sum of twenty thousand pounds (£20,000). The said Patsy Hill hereby further undertakes that she or her personal representatives shall pay any Inheritance Tax assessed in respect of such gift out of the assets of her general estate and indemnifies Raquel Holder accordingly.

Dated: 10th April 2020
Signed by Patsy Hill:
Signed by Raquel Holder:

Memorandum recording a gift where the transferor wishes the transferee to bear any Inheritance Tax arising

MEMORANDUM OF GIFT FROM
Scarlet Stewart of 15 Castle Street, Stirling

TO
Tanya Stewart of 42 Palace Road, Linlithgow

MEMORANDUM that on 20th May 2020 Scarlet Stewart transferred by way of gift to Tanya Stewart (subject to the payment of any Inheritance Tax) the sum of eight thousand pounds (£8,000) and IN CONSIDERATION of such transfer Tanya Stewart undertook to pay any Inheritance Tax in respect of such gift assessed upon Scarlet Stewart or her personal representatives and indemnifies Scarlet Stewart and her personal representatives accordingly.

Dated: 24th May 2020
Signed by Scarlet Stewart:
Signed by Tanya Stewart:

Note: it may be difficult for the transferee to sign the document at present, but this should be arranged as soon as possible. In the meantime, it is much more important for the transferor to sign, thus recording their intention to make the transfer a gift.

Immediate Exemption

While gifts to another individual should usually gain full exemption from Inheritance Tax after seven years, there are some gifts which can be exempted immediately.

Each person has an annual exemption to cover the first £3,000 of any gifts made in each tax year. Where the previous tax year's annual exemption has not been used, this can be used this year. Hence, most people will be exempt on the first £6,000 of gifts made. A couple making joint gifts of up to £12,000 will generally enjoy immediate exemption.

Where a gift becomes part of a regular pattern and is covered by surplus income not required to meet your usual standard of living, it may be immediately exempt as a 'habitual gift out of income'.

Hence, if you've just given your son £10,000, you may be able to make this immediately exempt by giving him £10,000 every year from now on. Well, it's up to you!

For lots more information on making tax-efficient gifts, see the Taxcafe.co.uk guide *'How to Save Inheritance Tax'*.

Chapter 44

The High Income Child Benefit Charge

An additional Income Tax charge is levied on the highest earner in any household where:

- Any household member has income in excess of £50,000, and
- Child Benefit is being claimed

The additional tax charge is equivalent to 1% of the Child Benefit claimed in the same tax year for every £100 by which the highest earner's income exceeds £50,000. Once the highest earner's income reaches £60,000, the whole of the Child Benefit will effectively have been withdrawn and the charge will have reached its maximum.

Those affected by the charge in 2019/20 or 2020/21 will have overall effective Income Tax rates on income between £50,000 and £60,000 as follows:

No. of Qualifying Children	Effective Tax Rate 2019/20	2020/21
1 Child	50.76%	50.95%
2 Children	57.89%	58.20%
3 Children	65.01%	65.45%
4 Children	72.14%	72.71%
Each additional child	+7.12%	+7.25%

As an alternative to the Income Tax charge, the claimant can choose not to claim Child Benefit. Families who chose not to claim Child Benefit in 2019/20 for this reason might wish to consider making a claim in 2020/21 since, in many cases, there is a strong chance income will drop, meaning the High Income Child Benefit Charge may not apply, or may not apply in full.

The highest earner's total annual income for the purpose of the charge is their 'adjusted net income'. This means taxable income less 'grossed up' gift aid and personal pension contributions, making these reliefs extremely valuable to individuals who are subject to the High Income Child Benefit Charge.

The effective tax rates shown above are for Income Tax at UK rates only. A further 2% needs to be added in respect of National Insurance on earned income received by individuals below state pension age.

An additional 1% should also be added for Scottish taxpayers (for example, the overall marginal tax rate applying to a self-employed Scottish taxpayer with taxable profits of £55,000 and four young children eligible for Child Benefit in 2020/21 is 75.71% (72.71% + 2% + 1%).

Different rates apply to dividend income, as detailed in Chapter 3.

Chapter 45

Using the Trading Income Allowance

One of my partner's daughters said she was going to start making fabric facemasks. She's just going to give them away to friends and family but it got me wondering: what if someone starts making something while they're in lockdown at home and begins to sell it?

This is where the trading income allowance may come in very useful.

An allowance of £1,000 per tax year is available to exempt small amounts of trading income. Where an individual's total gross trading income for the tax year exceeds £1,000, they may either deduct expenses as normal, or deduct the allowance from the total income.

The taxpayer may also deduct expenses as normal where this gives rise to a trading loss. As we saw in Chapter 36, the relief available for trading losses is quite versatile.

The trading income allowance can be used against casual income following the same principles. However, only a maximum of £1,000 of trading income allowance is available to each individual in each tax year (for example, if £600 is set against casual income, only a maximum of £400 can then be set against trading income).

The trading income allowance is not available on partnership trading income. Furthermore, the allowance is not available at all if you receive any self-employed trading income (as an individual sole trader), or casual income, from your own partnership or company.

NB: If you are making something to sell, don't forget Government guidelines on social distancing, etc, when the time comes to deliver it.

Appendix
UK Tax Rates and Allowances: 2018/19 to 2020/21

	Rates	2018/19 £	2019/20 £	2020/21 £
Income Tax				
Personal allowance		11,850	12,500	12,500
Basic rate band	20%	34,500	37,500	37,500(1)
Higher rate threshold	40%	46,350	50,000	50,000(1)
Personal allowance withdrawal				
Effective rate/From	60%	100,000	100,000	100,000
To		123,700	125,000	125,000
Additional rate		45%	45%	45%
Threshold		150,000	150,000	150,000
Starting rate band for interest and other savings income only				
	0%	5,000	5,000	5,000
Marriage allowance (2)		1,185	1,250	1,250
Savings allowance (3)		1,000/500	1,000/500	1,000/500
Dividend allowance		5,000	2,000	2,000
National Insurance				
Primary threshold	9%/12%	8,424	8,632	9,500
Upper earnings limit	2%	46,350	50,000	50,000
Secondary threshold	13.8%	8,424	8,632	8,788
Employment allowance		3,000	3,000	4,000
Class 2 – per week		2.95	3.00	3.05
Small profits threshold		6,205	6,365	6,475
Pension Contributions				
Annual allowance		40,000	40,000	40,000
Lifetime allowance		1.03m	1.055m	1.0731m
Capital Gains Tax				
Annual exemption		11,700	12,000	12,300
Inheritance Tax				
Nil Rate Band		325,000	325,000	325,000
Main residence nil rate band		125,000	150,000	175,000
Annual Exemption		3,000	3,000	3,000

Notes
1. Different for Scottish taxpayers (except on interest and dividends)
2. For married couples/civil partners if neither pays higher-rate tax
3. Higher-rate taxpayers £500, not available to additional rate taxpayers

Lightning Source UK Ltd.
Milton Keynes UK
UKHW021525070420
361446UK00003B/91